SO-ASE-821

EXPERIMENTS FOR FUTURE
METEOROLOGISTS

ROBERT GARDNER
AND JOSHUA CONKLIN

Enslow Publishing
101 W. 23rd Street
Suite 240
New York, NY 10011
USA

enslow.com

Published in 2017 by Enslow Publishing, LLC.
101 W. 23rd Street, Suite 240, New York, NY 10011

Library of Congress Cataloging-in-Publication Data

Names: Gardner, Robert, 1929- author. | Conklin, Joshua, author.
Title: Experiments for future meteorologists / Robert Gardner and Joshua Conklin.
Description: New York, NY : Enslow Publishing, 2017. | Series: Experiments for future
STEM professionals | Includes bibliographical references and index.
Identifiers: LCCN 2016025222 | ISBN 9780766081963 (library bound)
Subjects: LCSH: Meteorology—Vocational guidance—Juvenile literature. | Meteorology—
Juvenile literature.
Classification: LCC QC869.5 .G37 2017 | DDC 551.5078—dc23
LC record available at https://lccn.loc.gov/2016025222

Printed in the United States of America

To Our Readers: We have done our best to make sure all website addresses in this book were active and appropriate when we went to press. However, the author and the publisher have no control over and assume no liability for the material available on those websites or on any websites they may link to. Any comments or suggestions can be sent by e-mail to customerservice@enslow.com.

Photo Credits: Cover, michaeljung/Shutterstock.com (man holding umbrella), Harvepino/ Shutterstock.com (storm), Titov Nikolai/Shutterstock.com (atom symbol), elic/Shutterstock .com (blue geometric background throughout book), Zffoto/Shutterstock.com (white textured background throughout book).

Illustrations by Joseph Hill.

CONTENTS

INTRODUCTION

Meteorology is the study of the atmosphere, the layer of gases that surround our planet. Scientists observe air temperature and pressure, water content, air masses and movement, wind, and storms. Meteorologists are involved in weather, weather predictions, climate, and global warming. They use physics, geology, chemistry, and computers when trying to understand why the atmosphere behaves in the many ways it does.

Meteorologists are intelligent, imaginative, and creative. They enjoy analyzing and solving problems involving weather and the atmosphere. We hope this book will help you decide whether you would enjoy working as a meteorologist.

The basic requirement to become a meteorologist is a four-year bachelor of science (BS) degree in meteorology or atmospheric science. Advanced research, teaching, and management positions require a master of science (MS) degree or a PhD.

To prepare for a career in meteorology, you should take chemistry, physics, earth science, and all the math and computer courses offered in high school. Knowledge of computers and computer modeling are particularly important because weather predicting is based mostly on computer models that interpret vast amounts of data.

Also take courses in English and history that require writing because, as a meteorologist, you will have to write reports about your work and investigations. If you do well in these courses, obtain high scores on your SATs, and interact well during college admissions interviews, you will probably be admitted to a university where you can major in meteorology or atmospheric science.

To help gain admission to college, you could develop interesting and challenging weather projects for science fairs. These projects will provide useful information for discussion as you meet college admissions directors.

Once in college, you can major in meteorology. You will probably take calculus, physics, chemistry, and computer programming as well as meteorology, weather forecasting, and statistics. Other sciences will likely be required as well. If you want to be a TV meteorologist or weather forecaster, you should also take courses in journalism and speech.

During college, look for opportunities to assist in research, which you might find at the college, local labs, government agencies, or TV stations. Your adviser may be able to help you find such work as a volunteer or at a summer job.

With a BS degree in meteorology, you could find a job in the industry doing quality control or working as a research assistant. Or you could obtain a MS degree in education and begin a career as an earth science teacher at a high school. However, you might find it more rewarding to continue your education and obtain a PhD. This doctorate degree would prepare you to teach and to do research at a college or university or in industry. This path requires four to five years of meteorology and related courses after college, as well as research. You would likely be associated with a professor, helping him or her carry on research. It would also involve publishing some original papers, but your advising professor can suggest research that will lead to findings you can publish. If you are considering a graduate degree, make a list of graduate schools you might apply to during your junior year.

Once you have your PhD, you can find work with the government, industry, or a college or university. If you choose the academic path, you'll have more freedom to do research of your choice, but whatever path you take, be prepared to work hard for long hours. There will be competition and many challenges.

If possible, attend conferences on weather and meteorology where fellow meteorologists present papers and report on their research.

There are many jobs to choose from once you have a degree in meteorology. You might find employment with a government agency such as the Department of Defense, NASA, NOAA, or the National Weather Service. You might work for a TV station as a local weather forecaster, or on a national network, or for the Weather Channel. In any case, it would help to become certified. The American Meteorological Society can provide certification in various areas of meteorology including broadcasting and consulting. A bachelor of science degree in meteorology is required as well as examples of your work. You must also pass their examination.

In addition most entry positions require training. For example, the National Weather Service requires two hundred hours of on-the-job training per year for two years.

WHAT DO METEOROLOGISTS DO?

Most meteorologists specialize in one or more of the many fields that require their expertise. Some of those specialties include the following:

Aviation meteorologists study the impact of weather on air traffic. For example, icing, which can quickly cover a plane's wings, can greatly reduce a plane's lifting power. An aviation meteorologist would warn an airline if icing is anticipated at an airport.

Agricultural meteorologists study the effects of weather on crops and crop yields and the proper use of water, as well as the role of vegetation on weather and climate.

Environmental meteorologists are primarily concerned with air and water pollution and weather conditions that can spread or limit the pollution

Hydrometeorologists study the water cycle, rainfall, and rainfall statistics of storms. They predict precipitation, heavy rain, possible flooding, and flash flooding.

Nuclear meteorologists investigate the spread and distribution of radioactive particles and gases in the atmosphere.

Maritime meteorologists study weather at sea. They provide ships with air and wave forecasts and general weather forecasts for ships at sea.

Military meteorologists do research and apply meteorology to military purposes. For example, meteorologists were deeply involved in choosing the date and time for the invasion of Normandy during World War II.

Renewable energy meteorologists look for potential sites for renewable energy, such as solar and wind power, that would be practical locations for alternative energy.

Weather forecasters are meteorologists who forecast weather and collect data about the present state of the atmosphere. They use their knowledge of weather history, current atmospheric conditions in their area and surrounding areas, and computer models to predict tomorrow's weather and beyond. They also issue weather warnings when storms, such as tornadoes, hurricanes, and blizzards, threaten to cause damage and cause power outages.

THE SCIENTIFIC METHOD

Many meteorologists are involved in scientific research, seeking answers to questions they have. They ask questions, make careful observations, and conduct research. Different areas of meteorology use different approaches. Depending on the problem, one method is likely to be better than another. Developing a weather forecast, finding safer ways to use radiation, or searching for the calmest seas for a cruising passenger ship require different techniques, but they all have an understanding of how science is done.

Despite the differences, all scientists use a similar general approach, the scientific method, while conducting and reporting their experimental research. In most experiments, some or all of the following steps are used: making an observation, formulating a question, making a hypothesis (one possible answer to the question) and a prediction (an if-then statement), designing and conducting one or more experiments, analyzing the results in order to reach conclusions about the prediction, and accepting or rejecting the hypothesis. Scientists share their findings. They write articles about their experiments and their results. Their writings are reviewed by other scientists before being published in journals for wider circulation.

You might wonder how to start an experiment. When you observe something in the world, you may become curious and ask a question. Your question, which could arise from an earlier experiment or from reading, may be answered by a well-designed investigation. Once you have a question, you can make a hypothesis. Your hypothesis is a possible answer to the question (what you think will happen). Once you have a hypothesis, it is time to design an experiment.

In most cases, it is appropriate to do a controlled experiment. This means having two groups that are treated exactly the same except for the single factor being tested. That factor is called a variable. For example, suppose your question is: "Will a drop in air pressure, as measured on a barometer, be followed by stormlike weather?"

You might hypothesize that a drop in air pressure will be followed by a storm. You would watch the barometer frequently and look for a decrease in air pressure. If the drop in pressure was followed by inclement weather, your hypothesis would be confirmed. If there was little change in the weather, your hypothesis would be regarded as unsubstantiated.

Two other terms are often used in scientific experiments—"dependent variables" and "independent variables." The dependent variable depends on the value of the independent variable. For example, the area of a plot of land depends on the length and width of the plot. Here, the dependent value is the area. It depends on the length and width, which are the independent variables in this example.

The results of one experiment can lead to a related question. They may send you in a different direction. Whatever the results, something can be learned from every experiment.

BEFORE YOU BEGIN EXPERIMENTING

At times, as you do the experiments and other activities in this book, you may need a partner. Find someone who likes experimenting as much as you do. In that way, you will both enjoy what you are doing. **If any safety issue or danger is**

involved in an experiment, you will be warned. In some cases, to avoid danger, you will be asked to work with an adult. Please do so. We don't want you to take any chances that could lead to an injury.

Like any good scientist, you will find it useful to record your ideas, notes, data, and conclusions in a notebook. By doing so, you can keep track of the information you gather and the conclusions you reach. It will allow you to refer to prior experiments and help you in completing future projects. It may also serve as a reference point during the college admissions process.

SAFETY FIRST

Safety is important in science and engineering. Certain rules apply when doing experiments. Some of the rules below may seem obvious to you and others may not, but it is important that you follow all of them.

1. Have an adult help you whenever this book, or any other, so advises.
2. Wear eye protection and closed-toe shoes (not sandals). Tie back long hair.
3. Do not eat or drink while experimenting. Never taste substances being used (unless instructed to do so).
4. Do not touch chemicals with your bare hands. Use tools, such as spatulas, to transfer chemicals from place to place.

5. The liquid in some thermometers is mercury (a dense liquid metal). It is dangerous to touch mercury or breathe mercury vapor. Mercury thermometers have been banned in many states. When doing experiments that require you to measure temperature, use only electronic or non-mercury thermometers, such as those filled with alcohol. If you have a mercury thermometer in the house, **ask an adult** if it can be taken to a local thermometer exchange location.

6. Do only those experiments that are described in this book or those that have been approved by **an adult**.

7. Maintain a serious attitude while conducting experiments. Never engage in horseplay or play practical jokes.

8. Before beginning an experiment, read all the instructions carefully and be sure you understand them.

9. Remove all items not needed for the experiment from your work space.

10. At the end of every activity, clean all materials used and put them away. Then wash your hands thoroughly with soap and water.

The chapters that follow contain experiments and information that every future young meteorologist should know. Meteorology, however, is a vast subject and this book's limited space will allow us to touch only briefly on a few of the ideas and experiments that we trust will give you a sense of what interests you might pursue as a meteorologist. Let's get to work!

CHAPTER ONE

WATER, WATER, EVERYWHERE

Meteorology and weather cannot exist without water. Earth's surface of 504 million square kilometers (197 million square miles) is covered by a vast amount of water—1.37 billion cubic kilometers (328 million cu mi) of it. However, 97 percent of that water (1.32 billion cu km or 317 million cu mi) is ocean water, which is 3.5 percent salt. Humans cannot drink sea water. The salt concentration in our body fluids is much less than 3.5 percent. Sea water will "pull" water out of our bodies. It causes our tissues to dehydrate. The living cells of many of the plants we grow for food have about the same salt concentration as human cells. Consequently, these plants cannot grow in salt water or salty soil.

Fresh water makes up only 46 million cubic kilometers (11 million cu mi) or 3 percent of Earth's water. Most of it exists as ice near Earth's poles. Table 1 reveals where Earth's water is found.

Table 1: The location and quantity of Earth's water.

Location	Quantity (cubic kilometers	Quantity (cubic miles)	Percentage of Earth's Water
Oceans (salt water)	1,320,000,0000	317,000,000	96.6
Polar regions (ice)	37,530,000	9,000,000	2.7
Underground and available	4,170,000	1,000,000	0.3
Underground and unavailable	4,170,000	1,000,000	0.3
Lakes and ponds	125,000	30,000	0.009
Soil	66,700	16,000	0.005
Atmosphere	12,900	3,100	0.0009
Rivers	1,250	300	0.00009
TOTAL	**1,367,000,000**	**328,000,000**	**100**

EXPERIMENT 1

DIVIDING UP EARTH'S WATER

The distribution of Earth's water is shown in Table 1. By doing this miniature model, you will get a better sense of how Earth's water is divided. You will separate much smaller volumes into the same fractional parts shown in Table 1.

THINGS YOU WILL NEED

- **metric measuring cup or 1-liter soda bottle**
- **pail or dishpan**
- **eyedropper**
- **graduated medicine cup**
- **cup**
- **5 medicine cups, vials, or small paper cups**
- **saucers**
- **toothpick**
- **plastic wrap or waxed paper**
- **small stickers to use as labels**

1. Add 4.0 liters (4,000 mL) of water to a pail or dishpan. Let that water represent all of Earth's water.
2. Using a graduated medicine cup and eyedropper, remove 108 mL of water from the 4.0 liters. Put that water into a cup. That volume represents the water frozen near Earth's poles. Label it as such.
3. Using an eyedropper and a graduated medicine cup, remove 24 mL of water from the pail or dishpan. Put it in another medicine cup or vial. That water represents

the water under the ground. Only half of it (12 mL) is available for human use. Label it "underground water."

4. Again, use the eyedropper to remove seven drops from the pail or dishpan. Place those drops in another medicine cup or vial. The seven drops represent the water in Earth's lakes and ponds. Label accordingly.

5. Remove four drops of water from the pail or dishpan. Put the four drops of water in another medicine cup or vial. Those four drops represent the water in Earth's soil. Label as "soil water."

6. Remove one drop of water from the pail or dishpan. Put that drop in another medicine cup or vial. It represents slightly more than all the water in Earth's atmosphere. Label accordingly.

7. Finally, dip the narrow tip of a wooden toothpick into the pail or dishpan of water. Remove the toothpick and tap it on a piece of plastic wrap or waxed paper. Label that water—about 1/10th of a drop—as the water in Earth's rivers.

8. The water remaining in the pail or dishpan (about 3,864 mL) represents the water in Earth's oceans.

THE WATER CYCLE

Earth's water is in constant motion. We see water moving when raindrops fall, rivers flow, and ocean waves crash on beaches. But there is motion we don't see—the motion of the tiny molecules that make up water. Water evaporates (changes from liquid to gas) as it moves from lakes, rivers, puddles, plants, and the ground into the atmosphere. This gaseous water becomes part of the air only to condense and fall back to Earth as rain.

Earth's water moves in a cycle as shown in Figure 1. It falls from clouds as rain and then evaporates and re-enters the air. The quantities of water in various parts of the cycle are shown in Figure 1.

Earth's total water changes very little. It used to be thought that the volume of Earth's water was constant. But it was

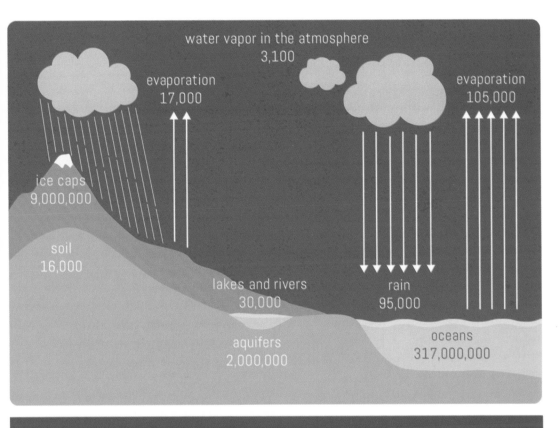

water vapor in the atmosphere
3,100

evaporation
17,000

evaporation
105,000

ice caps
9,000,000

soil
16,000

lakes and rivers
30,000

rain
95,000

aquifers
2,000,000

oceans
317,000,000

Figure 1. Where the world's water is found. Units are in cubic miles of water.

discovered that small comets carry snow into our atmosphere. The snow melts and vaporizes. Each comet carries about 20 to 40 tons (4,800 to 9,600 gallons) of water. Comets are believed to have added about 2,700 cubic kilometers (650 cu mi) of water to Earth over the last ten thousand years—a tiny percentage (0.0002 percent) of Earth's total water.

Because water is vital to life, we must take care to protect and conserve it. Water is being contaminated by pesticides, fertilizers, farm runoff, acid rain, and urban pollutants. Other than comets, there is no way to increase Earth's water so we must strive to protect and preserve what water we have.

EXPERIMENT 2

THE WATER CYCLE: A MODEL

1. Pour water to a depth of about 1 centimeter (.39 inch) in a glass or plastic pan that is about 5 centimeters (2 in) deep. The water represents the oceans, lakes, rivers, and all open water.

THINGS YOU WILL NEED

- **water**
- **ruler**
- **black plastic pan, such as the kind many frozen meals come in**
- **sheet of clear glass or plastic**
- **ice cubes**
- **bright sunlight or heat lamp**

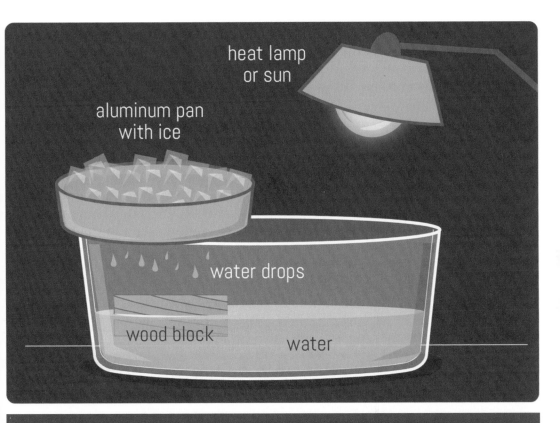

Figure 2. A model of the water cycle

2. Place a wood block at one end of the pan to represent land.
3. Cover the pan with a sheet of clear glass or plastic, which will represent Earth's atmosphere. If you use plastic wrap, tape it securely to the sides of the pan.
4. Fill a small aluminum pan with ice cubes. Put it on one side of the plastic or glass cover. It represents the cold clouds in the air above the water.

5. Put the pan in a place that gets bright sunlight or under a heat lamp (Figure 2).

6. After a few minutes, you will see water droplets condensing on the lower side of the cover that represents the atmosphere. You may even be able to detect smaller drops joining to form larger ones that fall back like rain onto the "ground" below or run down the side. If not, create some "thunder" by tapping on the pan.

Here is a fun fact: Roughly sixteen billion tons of rain fall on the United States during an average day. A trillion tons of rain fall on the Earth each day. That much rain, if collected, would occupy more than 200 hundred cubic miles (833 cu km) or about 7 percent of the water in the atmosphere. However, approximately the same quantity of water evaporates into the atmosphere. As a result, the concentration of water in the atmosphere remains constant.

EXPLORING ON YOUR OWN

- When ocean water evaporates, does the salt it contains go into the atmosphere? Do an experiment to answer this question.
- Build a model of your own design to represent the water cycle.
- Design and do an experiment to measure the energy needed to change one gram of liquid water to a gas.

EXPERIMENT 3

HOW RAINDROPS ARE MADE

As water vapor is carried up into the atmosphere, the air expands. When air or any gas expands, it cools. When their temperature falls, the water molecules move slower, making it possible for them to stick together. Some of the gaseous water may condense. However, atmospheric moisture may or may not form clouds, which consist of tiny drops of water. For raindrops to form, more is needed than cold temperatures. There must be tiny particles on which the water vapor can condense. These particles are known as condensation nuclei. Without condensation nuclei, water vapor can cool to temperatures as low as $-40°$Celsius ($-40°$Fahrenheit) without condensing.

Tiny salt crystals commonly serve as condensation nuclei. They are spattered into the air when ocean waves crash on shores. Updrafts carry the tiny salt particles with diameters of about one tenth of a micron (0.0001 cm) high into the air. It is there that water condenses on the particles, forming rain drops.

> ### THINGS YOU WILL NEED
>
> - **wide, clear plastic container that can be sealed**
> - **2 metal jar lids**
> - **warm water**
> - **table salt (sodium chloride, NaCl)**

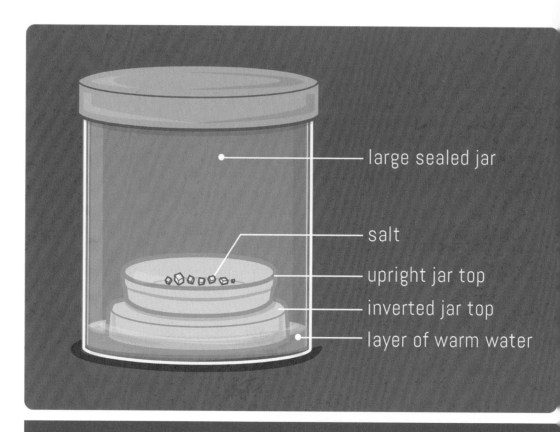

Figure 3. Will "raindrops" form on these salt crystals?

Will ordinary table salt crystals attract water vapor and form "raindrops?" Suppose your hypothesis is yes, raindrops will form. Let's investigate.

1. Find a wide, clear plastic container that can be sealed. Put a metal jar lid, open side down, on the bottom of the container (see Figure 3).

2. Cover the bottom of the container with a shallow layer of warm water. The water should not cover the metal jar lid.

3. Hold a second metal jar lid open side up. Add a few crystals of table salt to the second metal jar lid. Place that second jar lid on the first one as shown in Figure 3.

4. Add a top to the large plastic container to seal it. The warm water will evaporate filling the container with water vapor.

5. Examine the salt crystals every fifteen minutes. What happens to the crystals?

6. Do "raindrops" form? Was the hypothesis correct?

7. If raindrops have formed, remove the container's cover.

If the air outside the container is very dry, remove the lid with the salt crystals and watch the "raindrops." Do they evaporate, leaving the solid salt crystals behind?

EXPERIMENT 4

HOW BIG ARE RAINDROPS?

You can measure the size of raindrops. If rain consists of fine, gently falling drops, you can collect the raindrops quite easily.

THINGS YOU WILL NEED

- **rain**
- **cookie sheet**
- **plastic wrap**
- **metric ruler**
- **magnifying glass**
- **calculator**
- **pen or pencil**
- **notebook**
- **deep pan**
- **fine flour**
- **eyedroppers**

1. Cover a cookie sheet with plastic wrap. Then take it out into the rain and collect a few drops on the plastic.
2. Take the pan inside. Work quickly before the drops evaporate. The drops, as you can see, are tiny hemispheres.
3. Place a metric ruler beside a drop and measure its diameter. If the drop is very small, observe both drop and ruler through a magnifying glass.
4. Measure and record the diameters of a dozen or more drops.

5. The volume of the drops can be calculated from the diameter of the hemispheres. Table 2 gives the volume for a number of different hemisphere diameters. What is the average volume of the raindrops you collected?
6. In heavier rain, let a few drops fall into a pan that contains at least 2.5 centimeters (1 in) of fine flour. Each drop will form a dough pellet. When the pellets are dry, measure their diameters with a ruler.

Table 2: The volume of raindrops when the diameter of their hemispheres is known.

Diameter of hemisphere (mm)	Volume of drop (mm³)	Diameter of hemisphere (mm)	Volume of drop (mm³)
1	0.26	6	56.5
2	2.1	7	89.8
3	7.1	8	134
4	16.8	9	191
5	32.7	10	262

If you are thinking like a good scientist, you will say, "I doubt that the raindrops are the same size as the pellets." You are absolutely right! However, you can let drops of known size from eyedroppers fall into the flour and find the ratio between the diameters of liquid drops and flour pellets.

EXPLORING ON YOUR OWN

- Does the size of raindrops change during the course of a storm?
- Does the size of raindrops depend on temperature? Are drops of cold rain larger than drops of warm rain?

EXPERIMENT 5

HOW ACIDIC IS YOUR RAIN?

The atmosphere is mostly nitrogen (78 percent) and oxygen (21 percent). However, human activities have polluted the air with other gases. Growing amounts of carbon dioxide (CO_2) from the burning

THINGS YOU WILL NEED

- rain
- plastic container
- pH paper that can measure pH to at least ± 0.5
- a pH unit

of fossil fuels, as well as other greenhouse gases, are causing global warming. Gases such as sulfur dioxide (SO_2) and nitrogen dioxide (NO_2) released from the smoke stacks of many industries can dissolve in raindrops. These gases dissolve in the atmospheric water to form dilute sulfuric (H_2SO_4) and nitric (HNO_3) acids. When these acidic raindrops fall to earth, they seep into the soil and make it more acidic. They also fall on limestone and marble structures that slowly dissolve in weak acids. Acid rain entering soil, lakes, ponds, and rivers may kill the eggs and seeds of various animals and plants, which affects the food webs in these environments.

Acids form hydrogen ions (H+) in water. An acid's strength is determined by its pH, which is a measure of the concentration of hydrogen ions (H+). Neutral substances, such as pure water, have a pH of 7.0. Acids have a pH of less than 7. Substances that have a pH greater than 7 are said to be alkaline, or basic.

All rain is slightly acidic because atmospheric carbon dioxide, which makes up about 0.04 percent of atmospheric gases, is soluble in water. Dissolved carbon dioxide produces a solution that is slightly acidic so it is quite normal to find rain with a pH as low as 5.6. That is why acid rain is defined as rainwater that has a pH of less than 5.6.

You may be able to borrow pH paper from your school. You can also buy it from a science store, a science supply house, or a store that sells fish or swimming pool supplies.

1. To find the pH of rainwater, collect some rain in a plastic container.
2. Test the rainwater by dipping the end of a strip of pH paper into the water. You will need to use test paper that can measure pH to at least ± 0.5 pH units. Therefore, the paper should be able to distinguish pH 4.5 from pH 4.0 or pH 5.0.
3. Compare the color of the pH test paper dipped in the rainwater with the standard that came with the test paper. The comparison will show you the rainwater's pH. What is the pH of your rainwater?

EXPLORING ON YOUR OWN

- Is the pH of rain at the beginning of a storm different from its pH near the end? If it is, can you explain why?
- Does the pH of rain vary from season to season? Is it, for example, more acidic in the winter than in the summer?
- Is snow acidic? How can you find out?
- Is the pH of rain affected by location? Some people say that rain in the eastern United States is more acidic than rain in the Midwestern or far western United States? How can you find out?
- What other substances, such as smoke particles and engine fumes, contribute to air pollution? Design ways to detect some of these substances in the air.

EFFECTS OF ACID RAIN

Many lakes were normally alkaline at a pH of 8. When the pH fell to 7, concentrations of calcium in the water diminished. The eggs of some species of salamanders are so sensitive to the lower calcium concentrations that their populations are vanishing.

At a pH of 6.6 snails die; at a pH of 6 tadpoles fail to mature. If the water becomes more acidic, more life-forms die off. At a pH of 4.5, all fish die.

Acid rain falling on soil will dissolve chemical compounds containing mercury, cadmium, and lead ions, which are toxic. Microorganisms essential for decomposing organic matter succumb to these toxic substances.

CHAPTER TWO

WEATHER ELEMENTS

There are aspects of weather that we like to call weather elements, the basic factors that make up weather. These include clouds, wind, temperature, air pressure, and precipitation.

TYPES OF CLOUDS

Meteorologists classify clouds into three main types: cirrus, cumulus, and stratus. Clouds were given Latin names in 1803 by Luke Howard, an Englishman who watched clouds as a hobby. He later added another type—nimbus (from the Latin word for "rain cloud").

Cirrus (from the Latin word for "curl") clouds are thin, curly, and wispy in appearance. They are sometimes called mares' tails.

Cumulus (from the Latin word for "heap") clouds are the white, puffy, lumpy, fair-weather clouds commonly seen on warm summer days.

Stratus (from the Latin word meaning "stretch out") clouds are thin and layered. They often blanket the entire sky. Fog is a stratus cloud at ground level.

Today meteorologists use three prefixes to classify clouds according to their height. The prefix "cirro-" means high clouds at altitudes greater than 20,000 feet (6,100 meters). "Alto-" indicates clouds at middle altitudes of, 6,500 to 20,000 feet (2,000 to 6,100 m). "Strato-" means low altitude clouds, from ground level (as in fog) to 6,500 feet (2,000 m).

Using these names, you can arrive at the basic types of clouds found in Table 3 and Figure 4.

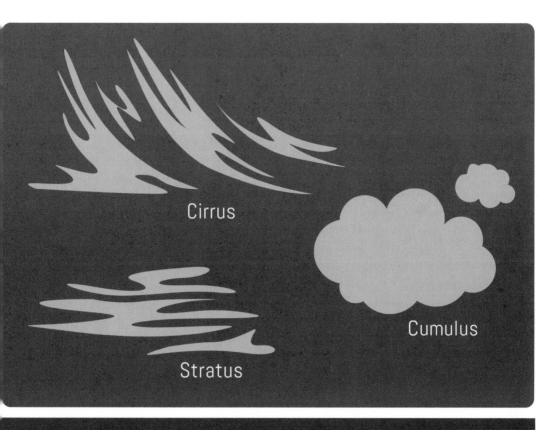

Figure 4. The three main types of clouds are stratus, cirrus, and cumulus. Others include cirrocumulus, cirrostratus, cumulonimbus, stratocumulus, nimbostratus, altocumulus, and altostratus.

Table 3: Types of clouds, their appearance, and the approximate heights at which they are found.

Type	Appearance	Height meters	Height feet
cirrus	thin, wispy, feathery	>6,000	20,000+
cirrostratus	layered, rain may follow	>6,000	20,000+
cirrocumulus	puffy, lumpy, fair weather	>6,000	20,000+
altostratus	layered, rain producing	2,000-6000	6,500–20,000
altocumulus	puffy, lumpy, fair weather	2,000-6000	6,500–20,000
stratus	layered, rain producing	0–2,000	0–6,500
nimbostratus	dark, layered, rain producing	0–2,000	0–6,500
stratocumulus	puffy, lumpy, often in dark patches	0–2,000	0–6,500
cumulus	puffy, lumpy, fair weather	low–2,000	low–6,500
cumulonimbus	puffy, lumpy, rain (thunderstorms)	low–12,000	low to 70,000

Cirrostratus clouds are thin and sheetlike and may cover the entire sky. Sunlight or moonlight shines through these clouds. The light may cause halos to form around the sun or moon. Cirrocumulus clouds are patches or sheets of white puffy or lumpy clouds.

Altocumulus clouds are like cirrocumulus clouds but appear bigger because they are lower and therefore closer to you. Altostratus clouds are gray or whitish sheets that cover the sky. A dim sun can be seen through these clouds.

Nimbostratus clouds cover the sky with a heavy dark gray layer. Stratocumulus clouds cover the sky with a deep, dark, and puffy gray layer. Cumulonimbus clouds are cumulus clouds that grow upward. They can become thunderstorm clouds and acquire an anvil shape at great heights.

Of course, you may see more than one type of cloud in the sky at the same time.

CLOUDS AND WEATHER

Clouds are the source of the rain that supplies plants with the water they need to grow and animals with the water they need to drink. Clouds are also useful in making weather predictions. Let's begin by making a cloud.

EXPERIMENT 6

MAKING A CLOUD

You may have accidentally made a cloud by opening a can or bottle of cold soda on a hot day. The cloud probably appeared briefly just above the bottle's opening.

You can make a cloud quite easily any time you want.

THINGS YOU WILL NEED

- **an adult**
- **clear, empty, 2-liter (67-oz), plastic soda bottle with screw-on cap**
- **warm water**
- **light background such as a window**
- **matches**

1. Remove any paper from the outside of a clear, empty 2-liter (67-oz) plastic soda bottle.
2. Pour about half a cup of warm water into the bottle.
3. Screw on the cap and shake the bottle to saturate the air inside with water vapor.
4. Hold the bottle up against a light background such as a window.
5. Shake the bottle again and squeeze and release the bottle. You will probably not see a cloud because one ingredient is missing—condensation nuclei.

6. **Ask an adult** to light a match, blow it out, and quickly drop the match into the bottle. There are now smoke particles inside the bottle.

7. Put the cap back on. Shake the bottle again and hold it up against a light background. Squeeze it to increase the pressure inside the bottle. Then suddenly release your squeeze. This will decrease the pressure inside the bottle allowing the air and water vapor to expand. You should see a cloud form.

8. To see another example of the effect of condensation nuclei, add a few crystals of salt to a glass of ginger ale. Watch a trail of gas bubbles form as the salt falls through the liquid.

EXPERIMENT 7

WINDS AND THEIR CAUSES

Wind is part of Earth's weather. A gentle breeze is welcome on a warm day, and a blustery day might be good for flying a kite, but winds of hurricane force can destroy lives and property.

THINGS YOU WILL NEED

- **a balloon**

1. To discover what causes wind, fill a balloon with air. Seal the neck of the balloon with your fingers. With your other hand, feel the balloon's surface. Do you feel an opposing force? Is the pressure greater inside or outside the balloon?
2. Put the balloon's mouth near your face. Slightly release your grip on the balloon's neck. You will feel a wind moving against your face. Why do you think air is flowing out of the balloon?
3. As you have just seen, air moves from high pressure to low pressure creating wind.

But what causes the differences in air pressure? It might surprise you to know that heat from the sun is at the root of wind. Heat is not spread evenly across Earth's surface. Tropical regions receive far more solar energy than polar regions. Consequently, tropical air is warmer than more northerly or southerly air.

As you may know, warm air is less dense (lighter) than cool air and exerts less pressure. Air having greater pressure will move into a region of lower pressure.

If we lived on a frictionless planet that did not rotate, air pressure differences alone could account for wind speed and direction. However, we live on a planet that turns and one where friction is common. As a result, there is more to Earth's winds than just pressure differences.

EXPERIMENT 8

WINDS ON A ROTATING PLANET

A rolling ball slows down and eventually stops because of friction. Friction is a force that opposes motion. Friction acts *against* motion. Air moving over Earth rubs against trees, grass, water, buildings, and so on. The air's velocity, like that of a rolling ball, is reduced by friction.

In addition to pressure and friction, there is something else that affects winds.

It is known as the Coriolis effect and it is caused by Earth's rotation. It was discovered by the French physicist Gaspard Gustave de Coriolis (1792–1843) in 1835.

To understand this effect, think about the ground at the North Pole. It simply turns in place. It has no velocity. It would be like you turning around in one place.

At the equator, the ground moves from west to east at a high speed. The equator is 24,900 miles (40,086 km) long and the Earth turns once every twenty-four hours.

Therefore, anything on the equator moves eastward at 1,038 miles per hour (1,670 kilometers per hour) because:

$$\frac{24,900 \text{ mi}}{24 \text{ hr}} = 1,038 \text{ mi/hr, or } \frac{40,086 \text{ km}}{24 \text{ hr}} = 1,670 \text{ km/hr}$$

To see how the Coriolis effect influences winds you can do an experiment.

1. Cut a piece of cardboard to match the circular top of a turntable, a lazy Susan, or a piano stool that can spin. Tape the cardboard to the surface on which it is placed. The center of the cardboard represents Earth's North Pole. Its circumference represents Earth's equator.
2. Use a moving felt-tip pen to represent the path of wind moving from the North Pole toward the equator. Draw a straight line (a radius) from the center of the cardboard to its edge. That is the path winds might follow on a stationary Earth.
3. Next, have a partner slowly turn the cardboard counterclockwise (west to east) as seen from the North Pole.
4. As the cardboard turns, slowly draw a *straight* line across its surface. Hold a ruler or yardstick just *above* the cardboard. The ruler will help you move the pen along a straight line. Keep the ruler fixed as you pull the pen along its side.

    How does this line compare with the previous one you drew? Why is the line curved relative to the cardboard? Did it curve to the right or to the left as it moved from pole to equator?

5. Repeat the experiment on a turning "Earth." This time draw a straight line from the edge (Equator) of the circle to the center (North Pole). Again, you'll see that the line is curved and seems to bend. Did it bend toward the right or the left as it moved? Why do the straight lines that you drew appear as curved lines on the rotating cardboard?

Winds moving across Earth's Northern Hemisphere appear to bend to the right just as the pen did when you pulled it in a straight line across the rotating disk. In the Southern Hemisphere, the winds bend to the left. Can you explain why?

Water currents in the ocean, such as the Gulf Stream that flows northward from the Gulf of Mexico, also bend because of Earth's rotation. Both winds and ocean currents bend to the right in the Northern Hemisphere (to the left in the southern hemisphere).

Wind directions are affected by the Coriolis effect as well as air pressure differences. As a result, winds in the Northern Hemisphere move clockwise about a high pressure center. They move counterclockwise about a low pressure center. See Figure 5.

To find the direction to a high or low pressure center you can use Buys-Ballot's law: Stand with your back to the wind. Raise both arms so they are horizontal. Your right hand will point toward higher pressure. Your left arm will point toward lower pressure.

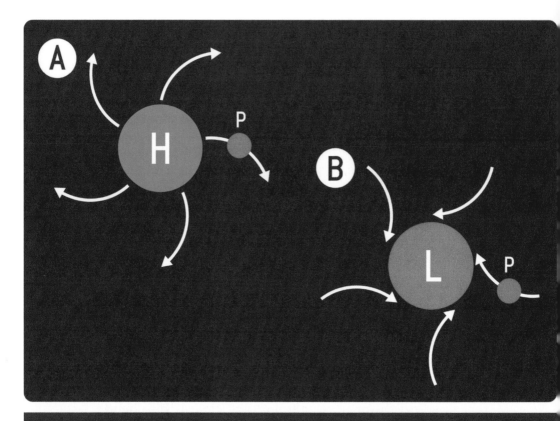

Figure 5. Wind moves away from areas of high pressure and toward areas of low pressure. Also, in the Northern Hemisphere, the rotation of Earth causes wind to move to the right. When these two factors combine, you can see that the wind at point P will move clockwise around a high-pressure system in (a) and counterclockwise around a low-pressure system in (b).

EXPLORING ON YOUR OWN
- Explain why Buys-Ballot's law works.
- There is a widely spread belief that the Coriolis effect causes water to always turn clockwise as it enters a drain in the Northern Hemisphere and counterclockwise in drains south of the equator. Carry out experiments to test this belief in the Northern Hemisphere.

RIDE THE JET STREAM

You have probably seen a picture of a wavy jet stream on a television or online weather report. Jet streams are narrow, fast-flowing air currents in the upper atmosphere or troposphere near the tropopause. Jet streams meander from west to east. The strongest are the polar jet streams at altitudes of 9 to 12 kilometers (5 to 7 mi) or higher. There are also weaker subtropical jet streams at 10 to 16 kilometers (6 to 9 mi) above Earth. Both of earth's hemispheres have polar and subtropical jet streams.

Jet streams are produced by a rotating earth and heating of air masses by solar energy. They form near the boundaries of warm and cold air masses and move west to east along a meandering path. They are a few hundred km wide with a vertical height of less than 5 km (3 mi). The velocity of the fast moving air in a jet stream may vary from 90 to 4,000 kilometers per hour (55 to 2,500 mph). The winds are the result of differences in air density, but, like all winds, the air is deflected by the Coriolis effect.

Your local television station will probably take note of any changes in the jet stream. If it shifts to your south, you can expect cooler weather. The north side of the jet stream draws in cooler air while the south side pulls in warmer air. So a shift in the jet stream can affect your weather.

EXPERIMENT 9

EFFECT OF TEMPERATURE ON EVAPORATION

The moisture in the atmosphere and, therefore, the rain that falls, comes from water that evaporates from oceans, lakes, and other places including damp earth. How does temperature affect evaporation? Here's an experiment that will help you to find out.

THINGS YOU WILL NEED

- **2 glasses**
- **cold water**
- **ice cubes**
- **hot water**
- **graduated cylinder or metric measuring cup**
- **2 aluminum pie pans about 5 in x 3 in x 2 in deep (12 cm x 7 cm x 5 cm deep)**
- **hot plate, food warmer, or stove**
- **thermometer**
- **clock or watch**

1. Fill one glass with cold water and ice cubes. Fill another glass with hot tap water at about 105°F (40°C).

2. Pour 100 mL (3 ounces) of the cold water (no ice) into a graduated cylinder or metric measuring cup. Empty the 100 milliliters (3 oz) into one of two aluminum pans. Set the pan aside.

3. Measure out 100 milliliters (3 oz) of the hot water and pour it into an identical pan. Place this pan on a

hot plate, food warmer, or stove. Adjust the heat to keep the water at about 105°F (40°C).

4. After an hour, bend one corner of the pan holding the cold water to make a pouring spout. Do the same to the other pan.

5. Measure the volume of cold water that remains by pouring the water into a graduated cylinder or metric measuring cup.

6. Then measure the volume of hot water that remains.

How much cold water evaporated? How much hot water evaporated? How does temperature affect the rate at which water evaporates? How might warmer oceans affect global rainfall?

EXPERIMENT 10

AIR AND WEIGHT

We live at the bottom of a sea of air that is more than 60 miles (100 km) deep. Most of the air is within 6 miles (10 km) of Earth's surface—less than 0.076 percent of Earth's diameter. Like everything else, air is subject to Earth's gravity. In this experiment you'll prove that air has weight.

1. Let all the air out of a basketball or soccer ball, but do not squeeze it together. Let it keep its round shape.

2. Weigh the ball on a balance. Record the weight.

3. Pump air into the ball until it is very hard. Then weigh the ball again. Record its weight when inflated. How can you tell that air has weight?

   Because air has weight, it pushes on everything it touches, including you. The pressure with which it pushes on an area of one square centimeter is about 1.0 kilogram of weight—a pressure of 1.0 kilogram-weight per square centimeter.

   (In the metric system, weight, which is a force, is measured in newtons. In this book we will use kilograms-weight (kg-wt) as our unit of force. A kilogram-weight is simply the weight of a mass of one kilogram, which, on Earth, weighs 9.8 newtons or 2.2 pounds.)

   Air pressure on Earth's surface is approximately 1.0 kg-wt/cm^2 or 14.7 pounds per square inch (lb/in^2).

4. To see the effect of this pressure, find an empty 1-gallon (4 L) metal can. Clean its inside thoroughly with soap and water. Then pour half a cup (118 mL) of water into the can. Leave the can's opening uncovered.

5. **Ask an adult wearing oven mitts** to put the can on a stove burner or hot plate. Let the water in the can

boil for several minutes. Steam will fill the can and push out the air.

6. **Have the adult** quickly place the can on an insulated mat or some newspapers. **The adult** should then immediately screw the cover back on the can or plug its opening with a rubber stopper. The steam, which has replaced the air in the can, will condense as it cools. This will reduce the pressure inside the can, creating a partial vacuum. Watch carefully for several minutes. What happens as the pressure of the air outside the can becomes greater than the pressure inside the can?

7. Here is another way to see that air exerts a pressure. Fill a test tube or vial with water. Cover the mouth of the tube or vial with a small piece of paper towel. Just to be safe, slowly turn the vessel upside down over a sink. You will find that air pressure keeps the water in the tube or vial.

With all that pressure from the air, why doesn't your body collapse in the same way the can did?

The reason is that the pressure inside your body is the same as the pressure of the air.

EXPLORING ON YOUR OWN

- Design a model to show why air moves in and out of our lungs when we breathe.

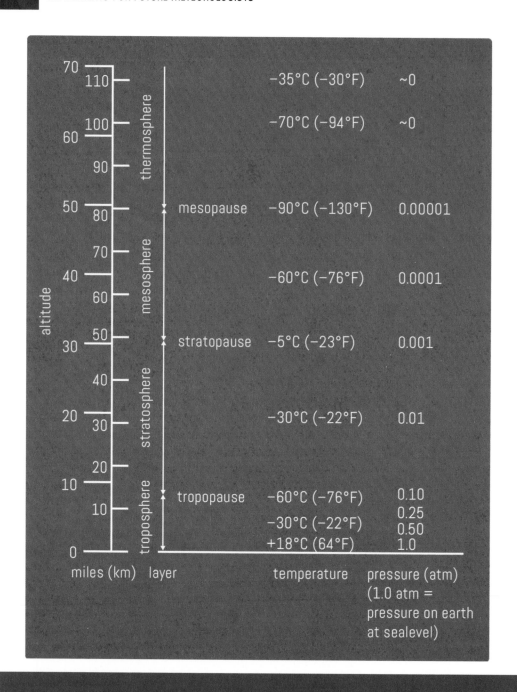

Figure 6. This chart shows how pressure and temperature change at different altitudes within the layers of atmosphere above Earth's surface.

AIR PRESSURE, WEATHER, AND A BAROMETER

Weather takes place in Earth's atmosphere. Most of what we consider weather occurs in the troposphere, the 6 mile- (10 km-) deep air closest to Earth's surface (Figure 6). But the troposphere is where we find clouds, rain, snow, sleet, hail, lightning, and all other weather phenomena.

Air pressure is very much a part of weather and weather predictions. Consequently, you should have an instrument that measures air pressure. That instrument is a barometer. It measures the weight of a column of air extending from Earth's surface to the top of the atmosphere. At sea level, that weight is equal to the weight of a similar column of water 10 m (32 ft) deep.

The world's first barometer (see Figure 7) was invented by an Italian physicist, Evangelista Torricelli (1608–1647). Torricelli filled a narrow 1.2-meter- (4-foot-) long glass tube with mercury. He put his thumb over the tube's open end (the other end was sealed) and inverted it. He then placed the thumb-covered end in a dish of mercury and removed his thumb. The mercury began to empty into the dish. It stopped emptying when the mercury level in the tube was 76 centimeters (30 in) above the mercury in the dish. This left an empty space at the top of the tube. Torricelli reasoned that the empty space was truly empty, a vacuum, because no air bubbles had come up the tube. He also reasoned that the pressure caused by the weight of the mercury pushing downward at the mouth of the tube was balanced by the pressure of the air pushing upward. (Air exerts pressure in all directions, up, down, and sideways.)

Meteorologists still measure air pressure by the height of mercury in a Torricelli barometer. A barometer with a mercury height of 76 centimeters (29.9 in) is normal air pressure at sea level. However, pressure is defined as a force per area (F/A). Can the height of a mercury column be expressed as a force per area? The answer is yes.

Suppose the open end of a Torrecelli barometer has an area of 1 square centimeter (cm^2). The volume of the mercury in the tube then would be 76 cubic centimeters (cm^3) because the area times the height would equal the volume of mercury in the tube.

area $\times$ height = volume, so 1 cm^2 $\times$ 76 cm = 76 cm^3.

Since 1 cm^3 of mercury weighs about 13.5 grams–weight (g–wt), 76 cm^3 would weigh:

76.0 cm^3 $\times$ 13.5 g–wt/cm^3 = 1,030 g-wt.

The pressure (force/area) exerted by the mercury would be:

$$\frac{1{,}030 \text{ g–wt}}{1.0 \text{ cm}^2} = 1{,}030 \text{ g–wt/cm}^2.$$

Since there are 1,000 g in a kilogram and 10,000 square centimeters in a square meter (m^2), we can also express the pressure in kilograms-weight per square meter:

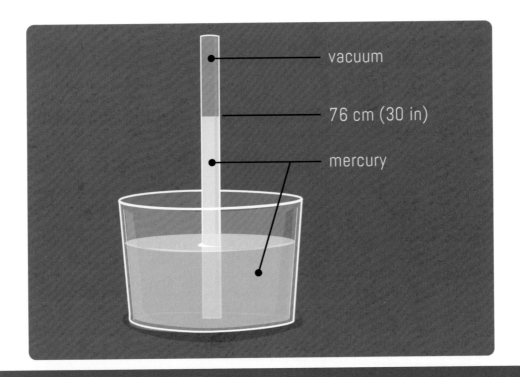

vacuum

76 cm (30 in)

mercury

Figure 7. This mercury barometer is similar to Torricelli's.

$$\frac{1.03 \text{ kg}}{0.0001 \text{ m}^2} = 10,300 \text{ kg–wt/m}^2.$$

Meteorologists often express air pressure in millibars. A millibar is the same as 1 g–wt/cm^2. In other words, 1 millibar = 1 g–wt/cm^2 and 1,030 g–wt/cm^2 = 1,030 millibars.

TEMPERATURE OF AN EXPANDING GAS

In Experiment 6, you made a cloud by suddenly decreasing the pressure on moist air by releasing your squeeze on the bottle. The pressure of rising air also decreases because there is less air the higher you go. When the pressure on any gas decreases, it expands. Does anything else happen when a gas expands?

THINGS YOU WILL NEED

- **thermometer**
- **spray can; an air freshener can works well**
- **notebook**
- **pen or pencil**
- **metal jar lid**
- **clear plastic container that can be sealed**
- **table salt (sodium chloride, NaCl)**
- **warm water**

1. To find out, hold a thermometer about a foot from the nozzle of a spray can. One that sprays an air freshener works well. The can should have been in the room for at least ten minutes so its contents are at room temperature. The vapor within the can is under pressure. It will expand when released.
2. Record the air temperature. Then press the nozzle button so that the expanding vapor strikes

the thermometer bulb. What happens to the temperature? What happens to the temperature of a gas when it expands?

EXPERIMENT 12

RISING, SINKING, AND DENSITY

Liquids and gases are both fluids, and, in many ways, they share similar properties. For example, both expand when heated and shrink when cooled. And, as you may know, a dense object, such as a stone, will sink in a less dense liquid, such as water. A stick of wood, on the other hand, floats in water because it is less dense than water.

> ### THINGS YOU WILL NEED
>
> - **2 vials or small glasses**
> - **cold and hot tap water**
> - **food coloring**
> - **eyedropper**

We can use warm and cold water to see what happens when warm and cold air meet.

1. Nearly fill a vial or small glass with cold tap water.
2. Place a drop of food coloring in another vial or small glass and then nearly fill it with hot tap water.

3. Fill an eyedropper with the hot colored water. Put the end of the dropper near the bottom of the vial that holds the cold water. Very slowly squeeze the hot water into the cold water as shown in Figure 8. What happens? Can you explain what you see?

4. Repeat the experiment, but this time color the cold water. Use the eyedropper to slowly squeeze the cold colored water into clear hot water. Can you predict what will happen? Try it! Were you right?

clear cold water

hot colored water

Figure 8. What happens when a warm fluid meets a cold fluid? When a cold fluid meets a warm fluid?

AIR MASSES AND FRONTS

An air mass is a widespread body of air that is much the same across its entire area. Its properties reflect the region of the earth where it forms. Air masses are classified according to where they originate: tropical (T), polar (P), and Arctic or Antarctic (A). Their moisture content is represented by continental (c) or maritime (m). Continental air masses form over land and are dry; maritime air masses form over water and are humid. When an air mass moves, it gradually changes. Air warmer than the surface over which it is moving is identified by the letter w. Air colder than the surface over which it is moving is identified by the letter k. What would be true of air masses identified by the letters cPk, mTw, cAw, mPw, and mTk?

A cold (k-type) air mass is often unstable. The cold air, warmed by the ground, rises and mixes with colder air above. A w-type air mass is more stable near the ground. The colder ground tends to keep lower air cooler and denser than the air above. This reduces upward movement of the lower air.

Fronts form where two different air masses meet. When a cold air mass overtakes a warmer air mass, it is called a cold front. When a warm air mass overtakes a cooler air mass, it is called a warm front. A stationary front is one in which warm and cold air masses remain side-by-side in one place.

The next experiment will show you what can happen when warm and cold fronts meet.

EXPERIMENT 13

AIR MASSES AND FRONTS: A MODEL

Remember, water and air are both fluids. Consequently, we can use warm and cold water to represent warm and cold air masses.

> **THINGS YOU WILL NEED**
>
> - **green and red food coloring**
> - **3 plastic medicine cups**
> - **freezer**
> - **small glass**
> - **warm tap water**
> - **spoon**
> - **clear glass loaf pan about 8 in x 5 in x 3 in deep (20 cm x 12 cm x 7 cm deep)**
> - **water at room temperature**
> - **cooking baster**

1. To see what happens when a cold front and a warm front meet, you will need two or three green ice cubes. This is easily done. Place two drops of green food coloring in each of three plastic medicine cups. Fill the cups with water.
2. Place the water cups in a freezer until frozen.
3. When the green ice cubes are frozen, fill a small glass with warm tap water. Add red food coloring to the water. Then stir until the water has a deep red color throughout.

4. Nearly fill a clear glass loaf pan with water at room temperature.
5. Once the water in the pan stops moving, remove the green ice cubes from their cups. Place them in the water at one end of the pan. What happens as the ice melts?
6. After some green water collects and begins to flow horizontally, use a cooking baster to slowly add the warm red water to the bottom of the other end of the pan as shown in Figure 9. What happens as a cold front forms? Can you explain why it happens?

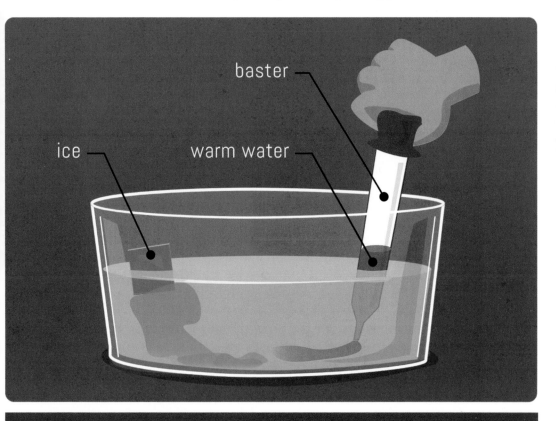

baster

ice   warm water

Figure 9. You can make a model to show what happens when a cold front meets a warm front.

EXPERIMENT **14**

WEATHER MAPS

The weather section of your local daily paper probably has a weather map similar to the one in Figure 10. The map will show you the location of high and low pressure centers as well as fronts, areas where precipitation can be expected, and high and low temperatures for major cities.

THINGS YOU WILL NEED

- **local daily paper or online weather maps**

1. Look closely at Figure 10. How would you expect the temperature in Minneapolis to compare with the temperature in New York City?
2. Read and save the daily weather maps from an online weather source or a local newspaper.
3. Refer to previous days' maps. In which general direction do air masses move across the United States? How can you determine the approximate speed at which a front, a high pressure center, or a low pressure center is moving across the country?

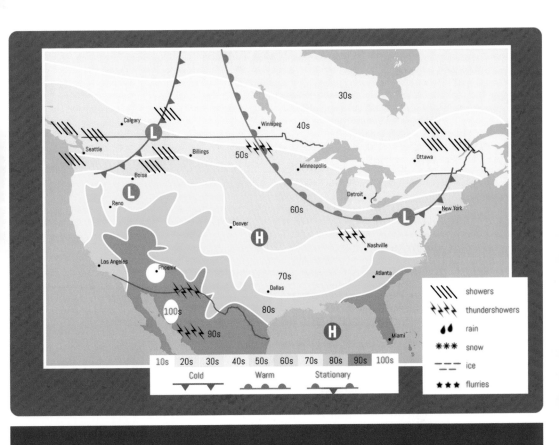

Figure 10. A weather map of the United States

CHAPTER THREE

BUILD A METEOROLOGY STATION

We want to make you as aware as possible about what is involved in pursuing a career in meteorology. To accomplish that goal we're going to ask you to build a small meteorology station. You'll begin by building and assembling the instruments meteorologists use to predict weather. Then you'll use those instruments to make weather predictions that you can email to your family, friends, and neighbors. You can become their local weather forecaster.

You can build most of the instruments you will need. Others may already exist in your home or can be purchased at a reasonable price.

Once you have assembled your instruments and understand how they work and what they measure, you can use them to record daily weather data.

The instruments you will need in your weather station are a thermometer to measure temperatures, a barometer to measure air pressure, a rain gauge to measure precipitation, wind vanes to find wind direction and speed, and a hygrometer to measure relative humidity. Later, you will learn how to measure dew points and calculate absolute humidity. The difference between relative and absolute humidity will be made clear at that time.

A THERMOMETER FOR YOUR METEOROLOGY STATION

You can use a household alcohol thermometer to measure temperature. **Do not use thermometers that contain mercury!** (See the safety section in the introduction.) It would be nice to have a thermometer that can measure the maximum (high) and minimum (low) daily temperatures. It would also be helpful to have a thermometer with both the Fahrenheit and Celsius scales. However, neither two scales nor the high-low feature is essential.

THINGS YOU WILL NEED

- **household alcohol thermometer, preferably one with both Fahrenheit and Celsius scale. A thermometer that measures maximum and minimum temperatures on a daily basis would be ideal.**

1. A thermometer is used to measure air temperature. It should be placed outdoors in a protected area that is shaded. A thermometer in sunlight will show a temperature higher than the temperature of the air.
2. If possible, measure and record the high and low temperature every day.
3. From the data you accumulate, calculate the average high and low temperature for each season. Then calculate the temperature range (from low to high) for each season.

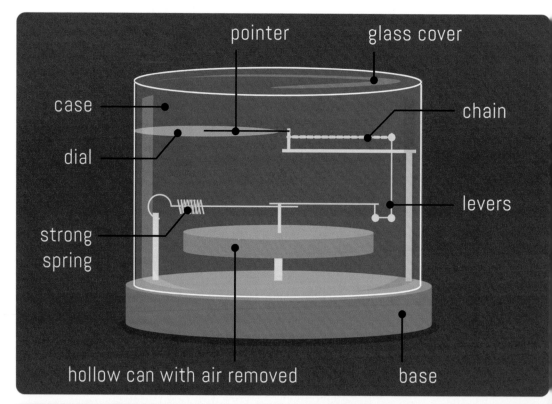

Figure 11. The hollow can in an aneroid barometer is squeezed by air pressure. Changes in air pressure cause the can to expand or contract. These changes are magnified by levers that are connected to a pointer by a chain. The pointer moves over a dial from which you can read the air pressure.

EXPERIMENT 16

A BAROMETER FOR YOUR METEOROLOGY STATION

Torricelli used a mercury barometer. Because mercury is expensive and its vapors are poisonous, you will use an aneroid barometer. (Figure 11 shows you what an aneroid barometer looks like.)

1. To see how an aneroid barometer works, use scissors to cut off the neck of a balloon.
2. Slip the remaining part of the balloon over the opening of a wide-mouth jar or a drinking glass. Secure it to the jar or glass with a strong rubber band.
3. Put two drinking straws together. Use scissors to cut one end of the straws diagonally to make a pointer as shown in Figure 12.

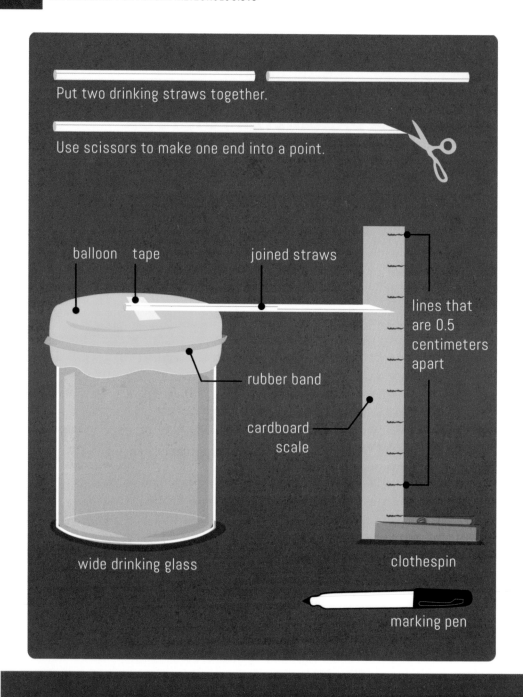

Put two drinking straws together.

Use scissors to make one end into a point.

balloon   tape   joined straws

lines that
are 0.5
centimeters
apart

rubber band

cardboard
scale

wide drinking glass

clothespin

marking pen

Figure 12. A homemade model of an aneroid barometer can be used in your weather station.

4. Using clear tape, tape the other end of the straws to the center of the rubber balloon covering the jar or glass.

5. Finally, use a strip of cardboard, clothespins, ruler, and marking pen to make a scale with lines 0.5 centimeters (1/4 in) apart. Place the scale beside the end of the pointer as shown in Figure 12.

6. Record the position of the pointer in your notebook. Look at the position of the pointer every few hours for the next few days. Be sure to look when the weather is changing from clear to stormy or vice versa. What do you notice?

   The balloon barometer you have built is a model of an aneroid barometer and will indicate changes in air pressure. As the air pressure increases, the rubber surface is pushed down and the pointer goes up. When the air pressure decreases, the higher pressure under the rubber surface pushes it upward and the pointer moves downward.

   However, for this barometer to be useful it must be kept at a constant temperature.

7. To see why, pull the mouth of a balloon over the top of an empty 1-liter (33-oz) plastic soda bottle.

8. Hold the bottle under hot water from a faucet. What happens to the volume of the air in the bottle when its temperature rises? How can you tell?

9. Put the bottle and attached balloon in a refrigerator. What happens to the volume of the air when its temperature decreases? How can you tell?

Why would your homemade barometer have to be kept at a constant temperature to measure air pressure?

The other problem with the barometer you made is that it can tell you only when air pressure is increasing or decreasing. It can't tell you what the pressure is in centimeters or inches of mercury, millibars, or any other numerical measurement.

An aneroid barometer is based on the same principle as the model you made. However, look carefully at the diagram in Figure 11. The hollow, metal drum, which corresponds to the jar or glass that you used, does not contain air. It is empty—a vacuum. Consequently, the drum's surface will only move in or out in response to air pressure. It contains no air that temperature would cause to expand or shrink.

You may have an aneroid barometer in your home. Sometimes you will find a barometer together with a thermometer and a hygrometer. If not, you can buy an aneroid barometer at a hardware store or online.

Keep the barometer indoors. The air pressure inside your home is the same as the pressure outside. No building is air tight. If the air pressure outside increases, air will move into your home until the two pressures are equal. If air pressure decreases, air will move out of your home.

EXPERIMENT 17

AIR PRESSURE AND ALTITUDE

As you go up into the atmosphere, there is less air above you. Therefore, you might expect air pressure to decrease as altitude increases.

To see if air pressure changes with altitude, take your aneroid barometer to the basement of a building. If possible, choose a building with three or more levels (a skyscraper would be ideal).

1. Read and carefully record the barometer reading at the basement level.
2. Carry the barometer to the top floor of the building. Again, read the barometer carefully and record the air pressure. Is the air pressure less as you go higher?
3. Carry the barometer up a tall hill. Is the air pressure less at the top of the hill?
4. Take the barometer on an automobile ride while you are a passenger. Compare air pressures at the top

and bottom of hills or mountains. Does air pressure decrease with altitude?

5. You might also take along an unopened bag of potato chips on an airplane trip. Feel the bag at low and high altitudes. What do you notice about the bag's firmness at the different altitudes? Can you explain what you observe?

EXPLORING ON YOUR OWN

- If possible, measure air pressure at different altitudes. Plot a graph of air pressure versus altitude. Can you use air pressure to measure altitude?

- Find the number of home runs hit in various major league ball parks. Would you expect there to be any relationship between home runs hit and the altitude of the ball park? Is there any relationship?

EXPERIMENT 18

A RAIN GAUGE: ANOTHER INSTRUMENT FOR YOUR METEOROLOGY STATION

Rain is measured by the depth of the water it produces in inches or centimeters. You can make a rain gauge, which is an instrument found outside a meteorological lab.

1. You will need a clear glass or plastic jar with straight sides (Figure 13). An olive jar works well.

2. Place the jar in an open area away from buildings, trees, and anything that might prevent rain from falling into it. You could **ask an adult** to wrap wire from a coat hanger around and under the jar to act as a holder. The end of the wire could be made into a hook. In that way the rain gauge could be hung from a fence.

> **THINGS YOU WILL NEED**
>
> - **an adult**
> - **clear glass or plastic jar with straight sides, such as an olive jar**
> - **wire coat hanger**
> - **tape**
> - **stake**
> - **drill and bit (optional)**
> - **ruler**
> - **clear ruler or ruler tape (optional)**
> - **marking pen**
> - **notebook**
> - **local newspaper**
> - **tall coffee can**

    You might tape the jar to a stake. Or you could **ask an adult** to drill a shallow hole slightly larger than the jar's diameter in the top of a post. The jar could be set in the opening.

3. After a rainfall, measure the depth of the water in the jar with a ruler. Or you can tape a clear ruler or ruler tape to the side of the jar. You might put a strip of tape on the side of the jar. You could then mark a scale on the tape with lines 1/4 inches or 0.5 centimeters apart.

4. After measuring the rainfall, record your measurement, empty the jar, and replace it. You can compare

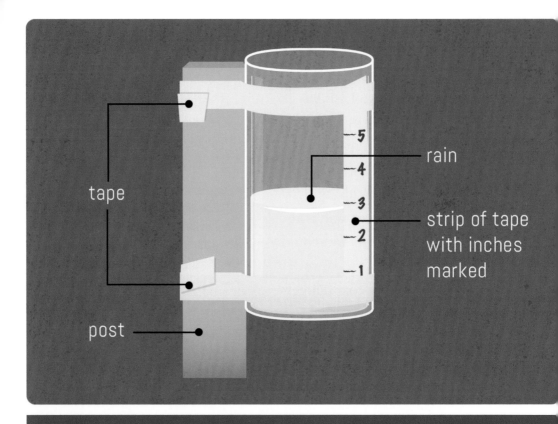

tape

rain

strip of tape
with inches
marked

post

Figure 13. You can make a rain gauge for your weather station.

your measurement of rainfall with one found in your
local newspaper.

Rainfall is important. Too much rain can cause
flooding; too little can result in a drought. Rain seeps
into the soil and enters the aquifer (the water in the
ground) or runs off into a stream or river.

Snow can be measured as rainfall, but 1 inch
(2.5 cm) of snow usually contains much less water
than an inch of liquid water.

5. To convert snowfall to inches of rain, first measure the depth of the snow.
6. Next, fill a tall coffee can with the loose snow. Do not pack the snow. Bring the can inside and let it melt.
7. Measure the depth of the can and the depth of the water (melted snow). From the ratio, depth of snow/depth of water, you can figure out the rainfall delivered by the snow. For example, if the can was 12 inches (30 cm) high and the melted snow was 1 inch (2.5 cm) deep, then a 2-foot (24-inch) snowfall brought the equivalent of 2 inches (5 cm) of rain.

    Don't expect the same ratio of snow depth to inches of rain to be true of each snowfall. Two feet of light fluffy snow might equal an inch of rain. On the other hand, 3 or 4 inches (7 or 10 cm) of wet slushy snow might provide an inch of rain.

EXPERIMENT 19

A WIND VANE

You can build a wind vane that will tell you the direction of the wind. Wind direction is defined as the direction from which the wind is blowing. A south wind comes from the south. Before building a wind vane and a device to measure wind speed, you might prefer to buy a simple combination weather instrument that measures wind direction, wind speed, rainfall, and temperature. You will find such an instrument in a number of stores as well as in mail-order catalogs or online retailers.

Wind measuring devices should be placed as high as possible in an open area away from buildings, trees, and anything that might prevent wind from reaching it. (Official winds are taken at a height of 10 meters (32 ft), but you need not be "official.")

Wind vanes are sometimes called weather vanes because changes in the wind direction often indicate a change of weather. As you observe the weather and record data provided by the instruments in your weather station, you will discover how changes in the direction of the wind can help you predict weather.

THINGS YOU WILL NEED

- **an adult**
- **piece of soft wood about 30 centimeters (1 ft) long, 2.5 centimeters (1 in) wide, and 1.3 centimeters (1/2 in) thick**
- **hand saw with a thin blade, such as a hacksaw**
- **heavy-duty aluminum pie or baking pans**
- **shears**
- **drill and bit**
- **finishing nail**
- **post**
- **plastic washer**
- **ribbon**
- **thumb tack**
- **small stones**
- **measuring tape**

1. To make a wind vane, **ask an adult** to cut a piece of soft wood approximately 1 foot (30 cm) long, 1 inch (2.5 cm) wide, and 1/2 inch (1.3 cm) thick.
2. At each end of the stick, use a saw with a thin blade, such as a hacksaw, to cut a 1/2 inch- (1.3 cm-) deep

slit. The head and tail of the weather vane's arrow will be slid into these slits and glued.

3. The vane's head and tail can be made from heavy-duty aluminum pie or baking pans. The tail should be a trapezoid about 3 inches (8 cm) wide, 7 inches (18 cm) long on one side, and 4 inches (10 cm) long on the side that slides into the slot. (See Figure 14.) The head of the arrow-shaped wind vane can be a triangle with a base of 3 inches (8 cm) and an altitude of the same length. The wide end of the arrow should be slid

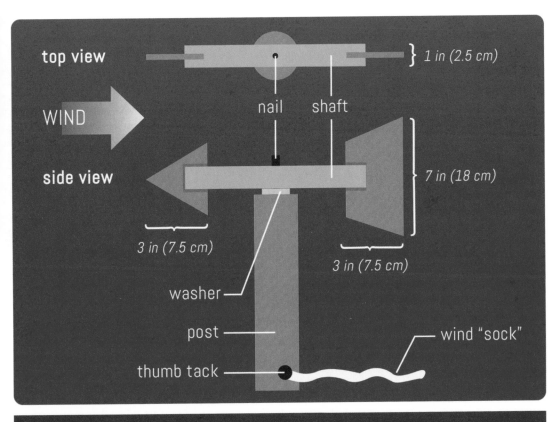

Figure 14. A wind vane

into the other slit that was cut in the wooden shaft as shown in Figure 14.

4. Balance the arrow on your finger. **Ask an adult** to drill a hole through the shaft at the balancing point. The hole should be slightly wider than the diameter of the nail you will use to fasten the weather vane to a post.

5. Place a plastic washer between the shaft and the post to which it will be nailed.

6. A nail can be used to attach the weather vane to a tall post. Put the nail through the hole in the shaft and the washer. Then hammer the nail into the post. Leave a space between the nail head and the shaft so the shaft is free to turn.

7. Tack a piece of ribbon to the post. The ribbon can serve as a wind sock like the kind seen at small airports. The wind sock will also detect the wind's direction. In fact, it may detect light winds that are too small to move the wind vane. How can you tell the direction of the wind by looking at the wind sock?

GETTING DIRECTIONS

Stand at the post on which the wind vane is mounted. If you can point to all the main directions (north, south, east, and west) you can easily determine the direction of the wind. If you don't know the directions, here's a way to find north. (Once you know which way is north, the rest is easy. Just face north, south will be behind you, east will be on your right, west will be on your left.)

To find north in the Northern Hemisphere, all you need to do is to find the shortest shadow of the post on which the wind vane is mounted. The post's shortest shadow will occur at midday, when the sun is highest in the sky and directly south. But midday is seldom at noon. The sun knows nothing about the clocks we use to tell time. Your best bet is to start marking the end of the post's shadow as the sun approaches its midpoint in the sky. You can mark the post's shrinking shadow by placing small stones at the end of each shadow. Continue to do this at five-minute intervals until you are sure the shadow is growing longer. Think of the mark that indicates the end of the shortest shadow as an arrow head. Think of the post as the tail of the arrow. The "arrow" points north. Knowing the north direction, you can identify all the other directions. Then you can easily find the wind direction by looking at the wind vane and the wind sock.

EXPERIMENT 20

AN INSTRUMENT TO MEASURE WIND SPEED

Meteorologists use an anemometer to measure wind speed. Their anemometers have three cups that catch the wind and rotate. The anemometer's spinning shaft turns a small generator that sends an electric current to the meter dial inside the station. The faster the wind, the greater the current.

You can make a different kind of instrument to measure wind speed,

1. You will need a piece of wood about 15 centimeters (6 in) square, as shown in Figure 15.

2. **Put on safety glasses.** Then hammer nails partway into two corners of the wood.

3. **Ask an adult, wearing heavy gloves**, to use tin snips to cut a strip of metal from a tall tin can. The strip should be about 1 inch (2.5 cm) wide and about 8 inches (20 cm) long. The adult can use pliers to bend one end of the strip loosely around a nail as shown in Figure 15. When you hold the instrument upright, as shown, the free end of the strip should rest on the other nail. A mark at the lower end of the strip can indicate a wind speed of zero. When the wind meter is pointed into the wind, the strip will be blown up at an angle.

4. To calibrate your wind meter you will need a car, a calm day (little wind), and **an adult driver**. Find a straight road where there is very little traffic. Ask your driver to go exactly 10 miles per hour (16 km/hr). Hold

THINGS YOU WILL NEED

- **an adult**
- **safety glasses**
- **piece of wood about 15 centimeters (6 in) square**
- **hammer**
- **nails**
- **heavy gloves**
- **tin snips**
- **tall tin can**
- **pliers**
- **car**
- **road with little traffic**
- **marking pen**
- **Beaufort scale (Table 4)**

Table 4: The Beaufort Scale: Finding Wind Speed by Observing Surroundings

Beaufort Number	Wind	Wind Speed (mph)	(kph)	Visual Observations
0	calm	0	0	Smoke rises vertically
1	light air	1–3	2–5	Wind direction given by smoke but not by wind vane.
2	light breeze	4–7	6–12	Leaves rustle; wind vane moves; can feel wind on face.
3	gentle breeze	8–12	13–19	Wind extends small flags; leaves in constant motion.
4	moderate breeze	13–18	20–29	Small branches move; dust and loose paper lifted.
5	fresh breeze	19–24	30–38	Small trees with leaves sway; wavelets form on lakes.
6	strong breeze	25–31	39–50	Large branches moving; utility lines seem to whistle.
7	near gale	32–38	51–61	Whole trees moving; some difficulty walking into wind.
8	gale	39–46	62–74	Twigs break off trees; difficult to walk against wind.
9	strong gale	47–54	75–86	Slight damage to buildings.
10	storm	55–63	87–101	Trees uprooted; considerable damage to buildings.
11	violent storm	64–74	102–118	Widespread damage.
12	hurricane	75+	118+	Extreme destruction of property.

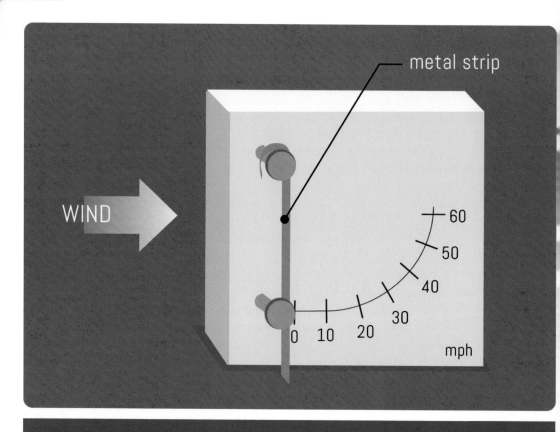

Figure 15. This device will measure wind speed.

the wind meter out the window so that the air pushes the metal strip away from the nail. Make another mark on the wood at the lower end of the metal strip. This mark can later be labeled 10 miles per hour (16 km/hr).

5. In the same way, make other lines when the car is traveling 20 miles per hour (32 km/hr), 30 miles per hour (48 km/hr), 40 miles per hour (65 km/hr), 50 miles per hour (80 km/hr), and 60 miles per hour (96 km/hr).

6. Test your wind meter on the next windy day by holding it so the wind pushes the metal flap. How much does the wind speed change from one minute to the next?

The Beaufort scale is another way to measure wind speed. It was devised by Sir Francis Beaufort (1774–1857), a hydrographer in the British navy. It allows you to determine wind speed by observing things in the wind.

Compare measurements on your wind meter with the Beaufort scale shown in Table 4.

EXPERIMENT 21

A HYGROMETER TO MEASURE RELATIVE HUMIDITY

Humidity has to do with the amount of water vapor (gaseous water) in the air. Absolute humidity measures the mass of water in a cubic meter of air. It is expressed in grams per cubic meter (g/m^3). You will measure absolute humidity later in this book.

THINGS YOU WILL NEED

- **2 identical household alcohol thermometers**
- **milk carton**
- **rubber bands**
- **scissors**
- **shoe lace**
- **water**
- **cardboard**
- **notebook**
- **pen or pencil**
- **Table 5**

Relative humidity is expressed as a percentage. It compares the amount of moisture (water vapor) in the air with the amount of moisture needed to condense into dew or a cloud. But more moisture can mix with warm air than with cold air. Consequently, the relative humidity might be 90 percent in the early morning when the air is cold and drop to 40 percent by afternoon when the air is warmer. The air over a desert is generally very dry and the relative humidity may be less than 10 percent. On the other hand, a rain forest is very damp and the humidity might be 100 percent.

To measure relative humidity, we make use of the fact that evaporation has a cooling effect. When sweat evaporates from your skin, it cools your skin. It prevents your body temperature from rising. To see this effect on a dry day or in an air-conditioned room, wet the end of your finger, then dampen your cheek by rubbing your finger across your cheek. You will immediately feel a cooling effect as the moisture evaporates.

The drier (less humid) the air, the faster water evaporates and the greater its cooling effect. Meteorologists have used this fact to devise a way to measure relative humidity. They use a wet-bulb, dry-bulb hygrometer, which consists of two thermometers. The instrument is also known as a psychrometer. One thermometer bulb is kept dry. It measures the temperature of the air. The second thermometer bulb is kept moist so that water evaporates and cools it. From the air temperature and the difference between the wet and dry bulb temperatures, the relative humidity can be determined.

This is done by using the information in Table 5. Of course, if the two thermometers have the same temperature, there is no evaporation. This means water is condensing as fast as it evaporates, so the relative humidity is 100 percent.

1. To build your hygrometer, find two household alcohol thermometers that read the same temperature when placed side by side. Attach the thermometers to a milk carton using rubber bands or tape as shown in Figure 16.
2. Cut a piece of shoe lace about 15 centimeters (6 in) long. Slip the open end over one thermometer bulb.
3. Make a hole in the carton near the lace. Push the lace through the hole so that it rests on the bottom of the carton.
4. Add water to the carton so that the lace is wet. Water will ascend the lace by capillary action. This will keep the bulb wet so that it will be cooled as water evaporates.
5. To use your hygrometer to measure humidity, fan the wet bulb for five minutes with a piece of cardboard, then quickly read the temperatures on both thermometers.
6. Record the temperatures in your notebook. Subtract the wet bulb temperature reading from the dry bulb reading to find the temperature difference.
7. Use Table 5 to find the relative humidity. First, find the temperature closest to the dry bulb temperature at the left side of the table.

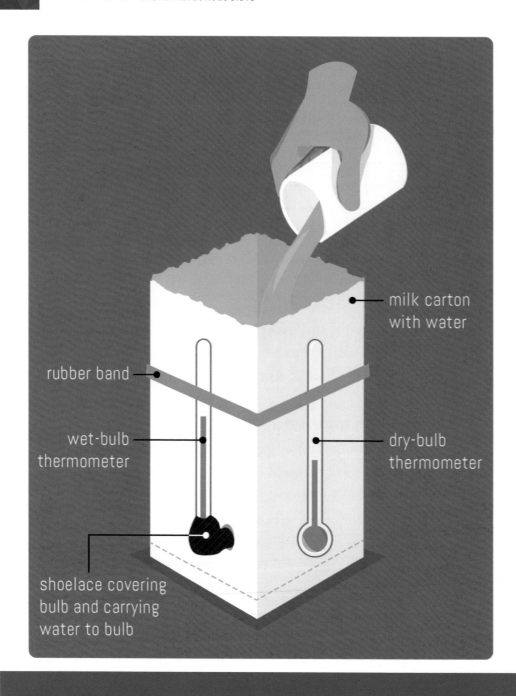

milk carton with water

rubber band

wet-bulb thermometer

dry-bulb thermometer

shoelace covering bulb and carrying water to bulb

Figure 16. You can make a hygrometer to measure relative humidity.

Table 5: Finding the Relative Humidity (percent) Using Fahrenheit Temperatures.

Dry bulb temp °F   Temperature difference in °F (dry bulb temp — wet bulb temp)

	1	2	3	4	5	6	7	8	9	10	11	12	13	14	15	16	17	18	19	20	25
35			91	81	72	63	54	45	36	27	19	10									
40			92	83	75	68	60	52	45	37	29	22	15								
45			93	86	78	71	64	57	51	44	38	31	25	18	12						
50	93	87	80	74	67	61	55	49	43	38	32	27	21	16	10						
55	94	88	82	76	70	65	59	54	49	43	38	33	28	23	19	14					
60	94	89	83	78	73	68	63	58	53	48	44	39	35	31	27	24	20	16	12		
65	95	90	85	80	75	70	66	61	56	52	48	44	39	35	31	27	24	20	16	12	
70	95	90	86	81	77	72	68	64	59	55	51	48	44	40	36	33	29	25	22	19	
75	96	91	86	82	78	74	70	66	62	58	54	51	47	44	40	37	34	30	27	24	
80	96	91	87	83	79	75	72	68	64	61	57	54	50	47	44	41	38	35	32	29	15
85	96	92	88	84	80	76	73	69	66	62	59	56	52	49	46	43	41	38	35	32	20
90	96	92	89	85	81	78	74	71	68	65	61	58	55	52	49	47	44	41	39	36	24
95	96	93	89	85	82	79	75	72	69	66	63	60	57	54	51	49	46	43	41	38	27

8. Next, find the number at the top of the table that matches the temperature difference between the wet bulb and dry bulb thermometers.

9. The relative humidity (percentage) is found where the dry bulb temperature row intersects the temperature difference column. For example, if the dry bulb temperature is 60°F (15.6°C) and the wet bulb temperature is 50°F (10°C), then the temperature

difference is 10°F and the relative humidity is 48 percent.

10. If you own or buy a sling psychrometer you will find it quite easy to measure relative humidity on a daily basis. You simply spin the wet and dry bulb thermometers until the wet bulb thermometer temperature is steady. You then read both thermometers to find the temperature difference and consult Table 5.

EXPLORING ON YOUR OWN

- If you have curly or wavy hair, you know that humidity affects human hair. Use that fact to build a hair hygrometer from a long strand of human hair that you wash and dry thoroughly.

You can also calibrate the hygrometer. To get 100 percent humidity, place your hair hygrometer in the bathroom while you take a hot shower. To get approximately 0 percent humidity, blow air over it with a hair dryer set on no-heat.

CHAPTER FOUR

WEATHER RECORDS AND WEATHER PREDICTIONS

Now that you have the essential instruments, you can begin to make and record weather measurements on a daily basis. This will allow you to see how weather changes on a seasonal, as well as a daily basis. It will also allow you to begin making weather predictions.

To help you get started, we will provide suggestions about keeping records. We will also help you use the instruments and records to make daily weather predictions. With experience your forecasts will become more accurate. Don't worry about making mistakes. Even professional meteorologists are correct only about 80 percent of the time.

As you begin making forecasts, you will find the most useful data comes from barometer readings, wind directions, and clouds. Increasing air pressure usually indicates the approach of fair weather. Decreasing air pressure often precedes a storm. West winds tend to bring fair weather, while winds from the south and east often carry damp air. Fluffy cumulus clouds are called fair weather clouds. Low stratus clouds that cover the sky tend to precede foul weather.

Again, don't be concerned if you make mistakes in forecasting the weather. Professional meteorologists have a great advantage over you. They are not limited to a single weather station. They receive data from many sources that extend from satellites orbiting Earth to instrument-bearing buoys in the oceans to other weather stations across the world. The data they receive is sent to computers programmed to analyze and model the information.

Twice each day weather stations around the world release helium balloons carrying weather instruments and a transmitter. The balloons rise into the atmosphere collecting and transmitting weather data as they ascend. The data is relayed back to weather stations. In this way the National Weather Service obtains information about wind speeds, temperatures, humidity, air pressure, and other weather indicators up to altitudes of 30 kilometers (19 mi). At such heights, the balloons expand so much because of the low air pressure that they burst and fall back to earth on a small parachute.

CLOUDS AND WEATHER PREDICTIONS

- Afternoon cumulus clouds indicate fair weather unless the clouds grow higher and become thunderheads, indicating thunderstorms by late afternoon or early evening.

- Patchy, high cirrus clouds in the west usually indicate fair weather. But if these clouds lower, thicken, and move from the south or southwest while an east wind is blowing at ground level, rain may follow within twenty-four hours.
- The fusion of high clouds moving from the south or southwest with an east wind at ground level may be followed by rain and a southwest wind within a few hours.
- Dark, lowering clouds moving from the south or southwest with southeast ground wind suggests steady rain is coming.
- Heavy, dark thunderheads with black bases growing upward indicate the approach of severe weather with possible hail and tornadoes. A weather warning should be issued.
- Cumulus clouds moving in the same direction as the ground wind and surrounded by blue sky indicate fair weather.
- You can anticipate foul weather if:
  - High clouds thicken and lower.
  - Fast moving clouds do the same.
  - Clouds develop dark bases.
  - The sky is filled with clouds moving in different directions.
  - Middle-level clouds darken in the west.
  - Heavy clouds grow upward on a warm summer morning.
  - Low-level, fast moving clouds are approaching from the east or south.

- Fair weather can be expected when:
  - There is a decrease in clouds.
  - Breaks appear in the clouds, particularly in the morning.
  - There is a ground fog that disappears during the morning.

MORE WEATHER INDICATORS

- Fair weather will likely continue when:
  - Air pressure is steady or rising.
  - The temperature is steady and normal for the season.
  - Your weather vane shows steady, gentle winds from the west or southwest.
  - The sun sets in a reddish sky.
  - Dew or frost is present in the early morning.
- A storm is likely when:
  - Air pressure is steadily falling and the wind is from the south, southeast, or east.
  - Decreasing air pressure is accompanied by wind from the east or northeast, indicating a storm approaching from the south or southeast.
  - A north wind shifts counterclockwise (from north to west to south).
  - The wind shifts to the south or east.
  - Temperature and humidity are both increasing and there is a south or east wind.

- The sun sets behind cirrus clouds.
- There is a ring (halo) around the moon.
- Clearing weather is likely when:
  - The wind shifts to the west.
  - Air pressure is rising rapidly.
  - Clouds are rising.
- Cooler weather can be expected when:
  - Air pressure rises.
  - The wind shifts to the north or northwest.
  - Winter clouds break and there is a greenish tint in the northern sky.
  - Colder air is known to be approaching from the northwest or west.
  - The sky is clear at night and the wind is calm.
- Warmer weather is anticipated when:
  - Clouds cover the night sky.
  - The wind shifts to the south or southwest.
  - A warm front is approaching.

EXPERIMENT 22

KEEPING WEATHER RECORDS

A record of weather indicators is essential to understanding how air pressure, wind direction and speed, clouds, and temperature can lead to accurate weather forecasts.

THINGS YOU WILL NEED

- **weather instruments: thermometer, wind vanes for direction and speed, gauge to measure precipitation (rainfall), and aneroid barometer**
- **notebook**
- **pen**

1. In your notebook you might make the following headings: Some sample input is provided.

Date	Temperature (°C) a.m.	p.m.	Precip (in)	Wind Direction	Speed (mph)	Air Pressure (in)	Sky	Clouds
3/22	10	18	0	SW	16	29 R	O	none

Weather symbols like those in Figure 17 can be used to save space and time.

Notice that in the sample record there is an R after air pressure (29). It's a good idea to check the barometer again after an hour or two to see if it is steady (S), rising (R), or

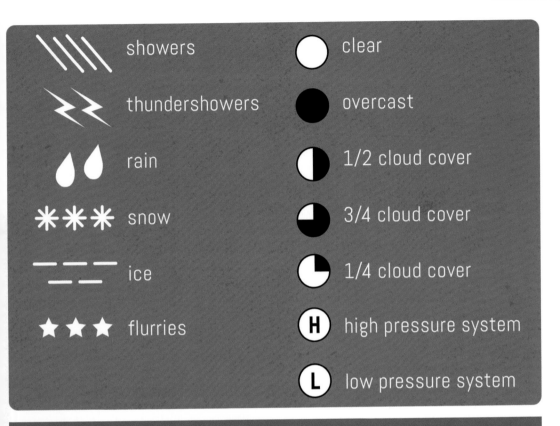

Figure 17. Some common meteorology symbols

falling (F). Changes in air pressure play a significant role in predicting weather.

WEATHER PREDICTIONS

From your own weather observations, you have probably found some clues that help you make forecasts. You may have discovered that clouds are valuable in predicting the weather. Here are some more things to watch for.

CLOUDS AS A KEY TO FORECASTING WEATHER

Cumulus clouds are often called fair weather clouds. However, if it is warm and humid, a cumulus cloud can grow into a cumulonimbus cloud. Violent updrafts of wind may lift the top of such a cloud to the tropopause. Such clouds are associated with thunderstorms.

Cirrus clouds usually appear during fair weather. However, if cirrus clouds are followed by cirrocumulus and cirrostratus clouds, a warm front may be ascending over colder air. Rain may follow within forty-eight hours. Halos of the sun or moon often appear with cirrostratus clouds. These halos can be a sign that precipitation is approaching.

Dark stratus clouds form when the air is laden with moisture. If thick and heavy, they usually accompany rain or snow.

BAROMETER READINGS

You may have noticed that when barometer readings indicate decreasing air pressure, rain or snow often follows. Remember, low pressure means air can expand. Expanding air cools as you have learned in Experiment 11. And cooling can cause water vapor to condense. A rising barometric pressure is a signal that fair weather is likely to follow. Do you see why? What would you expect if your barometer readings are steady?

COOL, CLEAR NIGHTS

Cool or cold temperatures near the dew point with clear skies and little wind are accompanied by radiational cooling. Heat escapes to the upper atmosphere at night. As a result, air near the ground becomes cooler. A cool, clear night might lead you to predict dew or frost for the following morning.

HUMIDITY

Drying air (lowering humidity) and increasing air pressure is a sign that fair weather is coming. Increasing humidity and decreasing air pressure suggests the opposite.

FRONTS

Approaching cold fronts may cause brief but heavy precipitation. Warm fronts are more likely to cause precipitation that lasts longer.

Warm fronts often mark the beginning of a storm and are accompanied by southerly winds. Sometimes they are preceded by fog. Cold fronts often follow a storm and bring north, west, or northwest winds.

DIRECTION OF APPROACHING WEATHER

Weather patterns generally move from west to east. If you know the weather to your west, predict that it will reach you tomorrow. A front to your west, northwest, or southwest is likely to reach you soon. Fronts to your east, southeast, or northeast will probably miss you. Hurricanes are an exception. They move east to west across the South Atlantic. They may turn northward as they approach North or Central America or as they enter the Gulf of Mexico.

Winds shifting to the north are usually followed by cooler temperatures. The opposite is true of winds shifting to the south.

WIND AND AIR PRESSURE

The forecasts in Table 6 are based on your barometer and wind vane readings. From what you know about fronts and high and low pressure air masses, see if you can explain why these forecasts make sense.

Of course, local conditions can affect the weather. For example, northern coastal cities experience a good deal of fog. Warm moist air in contact with cold ocean water holds plenty of sea salt particles (condensation nuclei). This condition is ideal for cloud formation at ground level. Areas on the west slope of mountains often experience considerable rain, while areas east of the mountains tend to be dry. Can you explain why?

ABSOLUTE HUMIDITY AND DEW POINTS

There is moisture (water vapor) in the air. That moisture is our source of rain. Only so much moisture (water vapor)

Table 6: Forecasts based on simultaneous wind vane and barometer readings.

Wind Vane Reading	Barometer Reading	Forecast
W, SW, or NW	High, rising fast	Fair and warmer, precipitation possible in forty-eight hrs
W, SW, or NW	High, rising slowly	Fair, temperature steady for next day or two
W, SW, or NW	High, falling slowly	Fair, temperature rising slowly for next day or two
E, NE, or N	Low, falling fast	Windy, precipitation likely
S, SE, or E	Low, falling fast	Windy, precipitation likely
S or SW	Low, rising slowly	Fair, clearing if cloudy and remaining so for forty-eight hours
Turning to W	Low, rising fast	Clearing if cloudy, lower temperatures
E or NE	Falling slowly	Precipitation likely by next day
SE, E, or NE	Falling slowly	Precipitation likely by next day

will mix with air at a given temperature. Sometimes air is saturated with water vapor. This happens when the amount of water condensing from the air equals the amount evaporating into the air. But unless it is raining, the air is not usually saturated.

The actual amount of water in a cubic meter of air is the absolute humidity. As you may know, the relative humidity is the ratio of the moisture in the air to the total amount that could be mixed with air at a given temperature. The maximum weight of water vapor in a cubic meter of air at different temperatures is given by the data in Table 7.

Table 7: The maximum amount of water vapor, in grams–weight, that can be found in a cubic meter of air at different temperatures.

Temperature		Maximum weight of water, in grams–weight (g–wt), that can be held by 1 cubic meter (m³) of air
°C	°F	
0	32	4.8
5	41	6.8
10	50	9.3
15	59	12.7
20	68	17.1
25	77	22.8
30	86	30.0
35	95	39.2

You can use the information in Table 7 to find the absolute humidity. But to do so you must first find the air's dew point.

EXPERIMENT 23

MEASURING DEW POINTS

You can find the dew point of air quite easily.

1. Add warm or hot water to a shiny metal can until it is at least half full.
2. Take the can and water outside. If moisture (dew) immediately appears on the can, use warmer water.
3. Place a thermometer in the water. Use the thermometer to stir the water as you add small pieces of ice.
4. Watch the outside surface of the can. When you first see dew (moisture) forming on the can, read the thermometer and record the temperature. That temperature is the dew point—the temperature at which the air forms dew.
5. Knowing the dew point, you can find the absolute humidity. Suppose you find the dew point is 59°F

(15°C). From Table 7, you see that a cubic meter of air at 59°F is saturated when it contains 12.7 g–wt of water vapor. Therefore, the absolute humidity is 12.7 g–wt/m³.

If the temperature of the air is 77°F (25°C), you can see from Table 7 that 22.8 g–wt/m³ would be needed to saturate the air. Consequently, the relative humidity is:

12.7 g–wt/m³ / 22.8 g–wt/m³ = 0.56 = 56 percent.

But suppose the dew point is at some temperature not listed in the table, such as 53°F. No problem! Use the data in Table 7 and the graph in Figure 18. The graph lets you interpolate between the plotted points. For example, if the dew point is 53°F, the graph would indicate that at 53°F, the maximum amount of water in a cubic meter of air is approximately 10.4 g–wt/m³. What is the temperature of the air where you are measuring the dew point?

6. Using the air temperature and the dew point, find the relative humidity. How does the relative humidity based on your dew point measurement and Table 7 compare with the reading according to your hygrometer?

7. How does the humidity inside your building compare with the humidity outside?

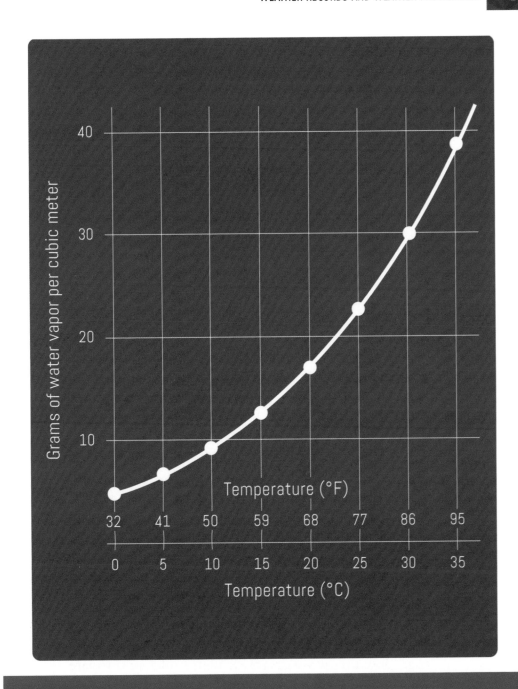

Figure 18. This graph shows the maximum amount of water that can be found in a cubic meter of air at various temperatures.

8. During which season of the year does the absolute humidity tend to be highest? When is it lowest? When is the relative humidity highest? Lowest? During which season of the year is the air driest inside your home or school? Under what conditions are you unable to determine the dew point?

The weather channel always reports the dew point so you can obtain it from there. However, you should measure the dew point occasionally, especially when the air feels very dry or very damp. Then compare your measurement with those from weather channels.

EXPLORING ON YOUR OWN

- Do an experiment to show why you should use a metal rather than a plastic or glass container to find the dew point.
- Do some research to find out how the data in Table 7 was obtained.
- Add crushed ice to the can you used in Experiment 20 until it is about one-third full. Add an equal volume of table salt and stir thoroughly to mix the salt and ice. Place a thermometer in the salt-ice mixture. Watch the side of the can very carefully. Do you see frost collecting? Do you first see dew that freezes, or does the frost form without first becoming a liquid (dew)? What have you learned about the formation of frost?

A WEATHER FORECAST BASED ON DEW POINTS

If you measure dew points frequently in the summer, you can issue a weather report about air comfort. When dew points reach 70°F (21°C), the humid air feels oppressive. Dew points between 60°F (15°C) and 70°F will cause many people to feel uncomfortable even when temperatures are in the 60s or 70s. Air with dew points below 60°F is generally considered comfortable.

EXPERIMENT 24

EASY-TO-MAKE PREDICTIONS

You can make morning and afternoon predictions about how warm or cold people will feel when outdoors.

THINGS YOU WILL NEED

- **thermometer**
- **hygrometer**
- **Tables 8 and 9**
- **wind speed instrument**

1. Here's a short summer weather report you can make. Measure the temperature and humidity. Then refer to Table 8 (the Heat Index). Now you can predict how the weather will feel in terms of temperature.

From the table, you can see that low humidity may cause people to sense that it is cooler than the actual temperature. On the other hand, with high humidity, people will feel it is warmer than their thermometers indicate.

Table 8: The Heat Index: Read down the left hand column until you reach the relative humidity measurement you made. Then read across until you come to the column that contains the air temperature. The temperature you find in that column will tell you how warm the air actually feels to the average person. When the heat index reaches 105°F, sunstroke and heat exhaustion are likely, so issue a warning.

Relative Humidity (%)	Air Temperature (°F)										
	70	75	80	85	90	95	100	105	110	115	120
	What the temperature feels like										
10	65	70	75	80	85	90	95	100	105	111	116
20	66	72	77	82	87	93	99	105	112	120	130
30	67	73	78	84	90	96	104	113	123	135	148
40	68	74	79	86	93	101	110	123	137	151	
50	69	75	81	88	96	107	120	135	150		
60	70	76	82	90	100	114	132	149			
70	70	77	85	93	106	124	144				
80	71	78	86	97	113	136					
90	71	79	88	102	122						
100	72	80	91	108							

2. Your winter weather predictions can include how cold the air will feel because of the wind. After recording the wind speed according to your wind speed meter or Beaufort scale, you can estimate how cold it will feel outdoors. To do this, read the wind chill temperature in Table 9. If the wind chill temperature is −19°F (−28°C) or less, frostbite can occur in fifteen minutes or less. Such wind chill temperatures should lead you to issue a winter weather warning about the danger of frostbite.

Table 9: Wind speed affects the way the temperature feels. The top line shows the actual air temperature in °F. The vertical column on the left gives the wind speed up to 40 mph. For example, with a wind speed of 20 mph and an air temperature of 0°F, the wind chill (the way the temperature feels) is −22°F. Wind speeds exceeding 40 mph have little additional effect on how the temperature feels.

Wind speed (mph)	Air Temperature (°F)											
	40	30	20	10	5	0	-5	-10	-15	-20	-25	-30
	How air temperature feels because of wind (°F)											
calm	40	30	20	10	5	0	-5	-10	-15	-20	-25	-30
5	36	25	13	1	-5	-11	-16	-22	-28	-34	-40	-46
10	34	21	9	-4	-10	-16	-22	-28	-35	-41	-47	-53
15	32	19	6	-7	-13	-19	-26	-32	-39	-45	-51	-58
20	30	17	4	-9	-15	-22	-29	-35	-42	-48	-55	-61
25	29	16	3	-11	-17	-24	-31	-37	-44	-51	-58	-64
30	28	15	1	-12	-19	-26	-33	-39	-46	-53	-60	-67
35	28	14	0	-14	-21	-27	-34	-41	-48	-55	-62	-69
40	27	13	-1	-15	-22	-29	-36	-43	-50	-57	-64	-71

EXPLORING ON YOUR OWN

- Design and carry out an experiment to detect the tiny particles found in air. Then develop a way to find the number of particles per cubic yard or meter.
- You can capture and preserve snowflakes. You can then examine them under a microscope. Place some microscope slides on a thin sheet of wood, such as a shingle. Put the slides in a cold, protected place that is below 32°F (0°C). Put a spray can of clear Krylon lacquer in the same cold place. Once the slides and lacquer are cold, spray a thin coat of lacquer on each slide. Hold the wood sheet with the slides in the falling snow until a few flakes collect on each slide. Put the slides back in the same cold place overnight so the lacquer can dry. Bring the slides inside and examine them under a microscope. What additional experiments can you do using this technique?

THUNDERSTORMS

We'll end this book with a BANG!

Thunderstorms are common on warm, humid summer days. The warm, moist air rises, often pushed upward by another air mass. As it expands and cools, the water vapor condenses into a cumulus cloud. The heat produced by condensation warms the air adding fuel to the updraft causing the cloud to grow taller. Often the cloud takes the shape of an anvil (an upside down triangle) as its temperature becomes equal to the temperature of the air above it.

As the cumulonimbus cloud grows, strong updrafts keep raindrops from falling. Bouncing about in the updraft gives the drops time to grow larger. Eventually the rising air currents can no longer overcome the gravitational forces on the large drops. They begin to fall. Drops in the falling precipitation evaporate. This has a cooling effect, which makes the air denser so it continues to fall. This results in downdrafts that eliminate the humid updrafts, thereby cutting off the needed "fuel" supply. The storm destroys itself.

As you know, thunderstorms are accompanied by booming noises (thunder). For reasons not well understood, the top of a cumulonimbus cloud becomes positively charged while the lower side becomes negatively charged. Meteorologists do know that ice particles are necessary for electrical charging to take place. If the electrical potential energy becomes very large, charges (lightning) flow across the cloud. Lightning can also travel from cloud to ground. Charges on the ground are attracted to opposite charges at the base of a cloud. Consequently, tall objects are more likely to be struck by lightning because they are closer to the charged clouds. There is no limit to the number of times they can be struck.

Thunder is heard shortly after the lightning. The reason is that the air around the lightning bolt is heated to temperatures as high as 54,000°F (30,000°C). The heated air expands suddenly creating sound waves.

Sound travels at about 0.2 miles (.32 km) per second, while light travels at 186,000 miles (299,337 km) per second. How can you use these different speeds to measure the distance to a lightning strike?

GLOSSARY

absolute humidity The mass of water vapor in a cubic meter of air.

air pressure The force per area exerted by air.

anemometer An instrument used to measure wind speed.

barometer An instrument used to measure air pressure.

Beaufort scale A way to estimate wind speeds by observing the effect of wind on objects such as smoke, trees, leaves, and flags.

cloud A high concentration of small water droplets or ice crystals.

condensation The change of a gas to liquid.

condensation nuclei Tiny particles on which water vapor can condense forming water droplets.

Coriolis effect The effect of Earth's rotation on masses moving over Earth's surface. The effect causes winds and ocean currents to bend to the right in the Northern Hemisphere and to the left in the Southern Hemisphere.

density The mass of a sample of matter divided by its volume.

dew point The temperature at which air becomes saturated with moisture and begins to condense.

evaporation The change of a liquid to a gas.

fog A cloud at ground level that forms when warm, humid air moves over a cold surface. The droplets are very small—two to fifty microns (millions of a meter).

meteorologist A scientist who studies weather and the atmosphere.

precipitation Water deposited from the air as rain, hail, sleet, snow, dew, or frost.

pressure Force per area.

rain gauge An instrument used to measure rainfall in inches or centimeters.

relative humidity The mass of water vapor in a cubic meter of air compared with the amount it would hold if it were saturated with water vapor. It is usually expressed as a percent.

sling psychrometer An instrument used to measure relative humidity. It consists of two thermometers. One thermometer has a dry bulb; the bulb of the other thermometer is wet. The temperature difference between the two bulbs can be used to determine the relative humidity of the air.

thermometer An instrument used to measure temperature. It is commonly used in weather stations to measure air temperatures.

vacuum An empty space where the pressure is zero.

water cycle The movement of water from Earth to air by evaporation and back to Earth as rain. The annual mass of water evaporated and the annual mass of rainfall are equal.

weather maps Maps that use symbols and lines to indicate temperatures, pressures, winds, precipitation, and weather fronts.

weather (wind) vane An instrument used to measure wind direction.

wind The movement of air over Earth's surface. Winds spread warm and cold air across the world.

wind direction The direction from which the wind is coming.

FURTHER READING

BOOKS

Ahrens, Donald C. *Essentials of Meteorology: An Invitation to the Atmosphere.* 7th edition. Pacific Grove, CA: Brooks/Cole Publishing. 2014.

Barrett, Raymond E. *The Annotated Build-It-Yourself Science Laboratory.* San Francisco, CA: Maker Media, 2015.

Bright, Michael. *Weather Explained.* New York, NY: Rosen Publishing, 2015.

Miller, Ron. *Chasing the Storm: Tornadoes, Meteorology, and Weather Watching.* Minneapolis, MN: Twenty-First Century Books, 2014.

Moore, Peter. *The Weather Experiment: The Pioneers Who Sought to See the Future.* New York, NY: Farrar, Straus and Giroux. 2015.

WEBSITES

MetLink
metlink.org/experimentsdemonstrations
PDFs, videos, and links to more meteorological experiments.

National Geographic Society
nationalgeographic.org/encyclopedia/meteorology
Videos and interesting information from National Geographic.

National Weather Service Weather Forecast Office
srh.noaa.gov/bmx/?n=kidscorner_weatherexperiments
National Weather Service website with more experiment ideas.

CAREER INFORMATION

AMS

ametsoc.org/ams

The American Meteorological Society's website. With links and career information.

Big Future

bigfuture.collegeboard.org/majors-careers

A career and job-based website with a focus on college majors.

NSSL

nssl.noaa.gov/people/jobs/careers.php

The National Severe Storms Laboratory website. Descriptions of a variety of careers with other interesting links.

Science Pioneers

sciencepioneers.org/students/stem-websites

Links to various STEM career websites.

WITHMYDEGREE.org

withmydegree.org/can-meteorology-degree

Offers ideas for what you might do with a meteorology degree.

INDEX

A

acid rain, effects of, 31
air masses, 55, 56–57
air pressure, 45–47
  and altitude, 67–68
  effect on weather, 49–51
American Meteorological
  Society, 8
anemometer, 75
atmosphere, 6, 10, 18, 19,
  20, 21, 22, 23, 28, 43,
  67, 86, 93

B

barometer, 12, 49–51, 60,
  63–66, 67–68, 85, 90,
  92, 94
Beaufort, Francis, Sir, 79
Beaufort scale, 77, 79, 103
Buys-Ballot's law, 41, 42

C

clouds
  making, 36–37
  types of, 32–35
  and weather predictions,

86–88, 92
computer models, 6, 10
condensation nuclei, 23,
  36–37, 94
condense, 19, 23, 47, 80, 92,
  104
Coriolis, Gaspard Gustave
  de, 39
Coriolis effect, 39, 40, 41,
  42, 43

D

density, 53–54
Department of Defense, 8
"dependent variables," 12
dew points, 61, 93, 94–96,
  97–101

E

evaporation, 80–81
  effect of temperature on,
    44–45

F

friction, 38, 39
fronts, 55, 56–57, 93